A PRIMER OF HEALTH PROMOTION

Editor: Janis K. Oppelt
Art/Cover Design: Nancy J. Obloy
Typesetter: University Graphics, Inc. Atlantic Highlands, New Jersey
Printer: Cumberland Valley Offset, Waynesboro, Pennsylvania
Typeface: Palatino (text)
             ITC Bookman Medium (display)

A PRIMER OF HEALTH PROMOTION

Creating Healthy Organizational Cultures

Joseph P. Opatz, Ph.D.

Oryn Publications, Inc.
Washington, D.C.

A Primer of Health Promotion: Creating Healthy Organizational Cultures

Library of Congress Cataloging in Publication Data

Opatz, Joseph P.
  A primer of health promotion.

  Bibliography: p.
  1. Health education. 2. Health. 3. Preventive health services. 4. Hospitals—Health promotion services. I. Title. [DNLM: 1. Health Promotion. 2. Health Promotion—directories. 3 Organizations. WA 590 061p]
RA440.5.063 1985 613'.07'1   84-22715
ISBN 0-916207-09-9

ISBN 0-916207-09-9

Printed in the United States of America

86 87 88 89 90   10 9 8 7 6 5 4 3 2 1

CONTENTS

To my Grandmother Adeline Opatz

PREFACE

The convergence of important new social and economic factors has created a new view of personal health. The improved economic status of a growing number of Americans has resulted in more free time and a greater choice of lifestyles. Concurrently, an increased uneasiness about the ability of the medical community to further improve the health and well-being of the average person has contributed to the rapid appearance and growth of such grassroots phenomenon as the running and fitness movement, holistic health centers, the health foods industry, and emotional and spiritual disciplines such as yoga and Transcendental Meditation.

At the same time, and not entirely unrelated, major social institutions have expressed an interest in promoting and maintaining individual health. In addition to demands being made by their members, many organizations are under ever increasing economic pressure to improve individual health as a strategy to reduce the burdensome social and economic costs of disease.

Government, schools, and, in particular, employers are redirecting some of their resources from disease identification and treatment to disease prevention and health enhancement. The health promotion movement has evolved from the combined effects of institutional commitment and individual interest in improved health. This movement has created the need for new models and strategies for effecting the change of both the behavior of the individual and the environments of the organization with which individuals must interact.

Two important precepts of health promotion are the importance of self-responsibility and the influence of the organizational culture on personal well-being. In no small measure, the major social maladies are the result of individual lifestyle choices. But decisions to make new choices and, more importantly, the ability to stick to the choices made, are influenced by the social, psychological, and physical environments or cultures in which they are enacted. Successful health change programs will acknowledge the importance of both self-responsibility and the influence of culture as a means to improving the health of organizational members.

This book seeks to provide the basic ingredients necessary for the creation of successful, comprehensive organizational programs designed to enhance individual and organizational health. Though emphasis is given to the process of creating healthy cultures in the work environment, most of the concepts and strategies set forth are applicable to any organizational membership, be they college students, community members, senior citizens, or hospital clients.

FOREWORD

An organization's primary asset is the health of its employees. To maintain this health, employers must nurture a dynamic, growing relationship between these individuals and their work environments. Organizations that provide their employees with opportunities for personal well-being are making a wise investment in the future growth, and profitability, of their company.

In recent years, many issues of real concern, and real cost, to employers have developed. These include:

   –Escalating employee health care costs
   –Absenteeism
   –Low productivity and morale
   –Stressful environments
   –High turnovers

Management is often reminded of these issues when it is time to review its profit and loss statement. Employees become assets to maximize or liabilities to reduce. A corporation's financial health depends on healthy and competent employees for its profits—but for its losses, it can only blame itself and its lack of involvement in employee motivation and productivity.

Employers can use a variety of creative measures to curb these unproductive and non-profitable issues. Health promotion programs offer large and small companies alike the opportunity to control problems that contribute to losses before those losses take control of the company budget.

Such measures will protect, enhance, and/or rehabilitate. Employees, and oftentimes their families, can learn many things through health promotion programs:

   –Managing stress
   –Eating right
   –Exercise
   –Medical self-care
   –Controlling drug and alcohol abuse
   –Stopping smoking
   –Reducing body fat

The only limit to what a health promotion program can do is in the imagination of its creators.

Organizations that have made a commitment to promote and to maintain the health of their members will find Joseph Opatz's book a valuable guide. With an eye to the future, Dr. Opatz establishes a firm foundation of alternatives for organizations who have chosen the strategy of improving individual health in order to reduce the burdensome social and economic costs of disease.

As an informed advocate of the health promotion movement, the author presents a comprehensive strategy for changing both the behavior and the work environment of the individual. He lays out a plan that acknowledges the importance of an individual's culture—social, psychological, and physical—and integrates this culture into the permanent changes needed for improved health.

This book goes even one step further, it reinforces the notion that health promotion can serve as a powerful tool for organizational change—the greatest challenge any manager faces. I believe that this book provides a great opportunity to learn how to utilize the existing culture to the advantage of both the individual's and the organization's health.

Dr. Opatz has given his colleagues a valuable resource for establishing successful organizational health promotion programs. By presenting the basic rationales and components of a sample model, readers will learn how to design a program of their own, one that can aid in creating a healthy work environment. Before they're through, they'll realize just how much of an asset their employees can be to the organization.

George J. Pfeiffer

Vice President, Center for Corporate
    Health Promotion
Reston, Virginia

Former Director Xerox Corporation
    Employee Fitness Center
Past President, Association for
    Fitness in Business

ACKNOWLEDGMENTS

I wish to thank the Board of Directors of the Institute for Lifestyle Improvement, namely Bill Hettler, Fred Leafgren, and Dennis Elsenrath, for their continuing support of my work. Also, I am grateful to the Staff of the Institute and in particular Diane Dieterich for her diligent and competent manuscript preparation. Finally, a note of thanks to Earl Hipp with whom I first discussed some of the ideas for this book.

ABOUT THE AUTHOR

JOSEPH P. OPATZ received his BA from St. Cloud State University, an MEd from Kent State University, and his PhD from the University of Minnesota. He currently serves as the Executive Director of the National Wellness Institute, University of Wisconsin-Stevens Point, Stevens Point, Wisconsin.

Dr. Opatz' present duties include health promotion on a consulting basis to numerous organizations, including hospitals, universities, and corporations. The purposes of the Institute, under his guidance, are to provide national leadership in wellness and health promotion, to provide wellness and health promotion services, programs and products, as well as to provide educational opportunities on a national basis through the National Wellness Conference sponsored each year at the Stevens Point campus.

This book is the result of Dr. Opatz' research and experience in the field of wellness and health promotion.

— 1 —

Introduction: The Wellness Point of View

Our society has seen a remarkable increase in life expectancy as a result of health improvements. For most of the two to four million years of human history, average life expectancy was no more than 30 years. As recently as the fourteenth century, the average adult in England was likely to die before reaching age 40. Within a relatively short period of time, the human species, particularly in western societies, has seen a dramatic increase in life expectancy. A child born today will likely become an octogenarian.

Yet despite this dramatic improvement in longevity and overall health, a growing body of evidence suggests that we should be able to live even longer and better. There are examples of isolated agrarian societies in the world, such as the Soviet Georgians, that have life expectancies much greater than our own. Members of these societies frequently live to be 100 or more. Studies have been undertaken to determine how these centenarian cultures differ from American society. A number of factors common to these societies have been identified. Because they are agrarian, their primary sources of food are whole grains, vegetables, and very little red meat. They exhibit work patterns that continue well into old age and are exemplified by vigorous physical activity. In addition there is strong social support for family members, particularly the elderly. They achieve these extremely old ages in vigorous condition despite the lack of sophisticated medical care.

From a purely physiological point of view, evidence now shows that, as a biological system, we have the potential to achieve ages far in excess of 100 years. Theodore Reiff (1984) estimates that the age of 120 can be achieved before significant degeneration of body function need occur. It appears, then, that we in America seldom die of old age. Instead, a number of other factors impinge on our potential life expectancy and cause premature disease and death.

A significant impetus for the changing view of health in America has resulted from the dramatic shift in the ways we have been dying since the turn of the century. In the late 1800s and early 1900s the major killers were infectious diseases. Primary among them were pneumonia, flu, and tuberculosis. We now die from some very different ailments, chief among them, heart disease, stroke, cancer, and accidents. These new diseases, often called diseases of choice, are unlike the ailments of the past over which the individual had little or no control. The implication is that the current killers are, to a great extent, the result of individual lifestyle choices. Figures 1.1 and 1.2 contrast the causes of death in 1900 with today.

Despite this significant shift in causes of morbidity, we continue to address illness in much the same way we always have. Investment in efforts to treat and cure infectious diseases obtained significant results. Figure 1.3 shows the declining death rate per 100,000 and some important contributions to this decline over the course of the last century. Much of this decline is attributable to public health improvements such as cleaner

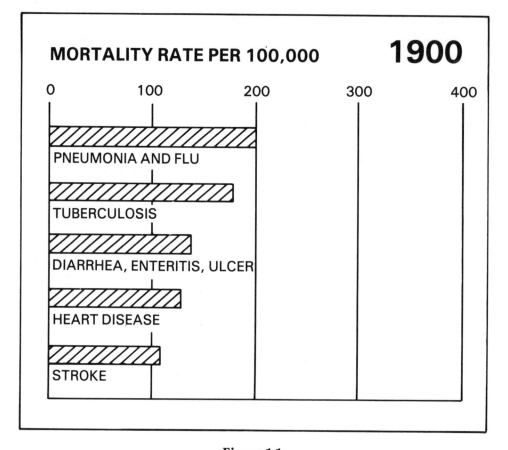

Figure 1.1

water, improved sewage systems, pasteurization of milk, and less crowded housing in inner cities. During the 1930s, 40s, and early 50s, came the discovery of sulfa drugs, anti TB drugs, and penicillin.

Interestingly enough, however, the dramatic reduction in death rates came to a sudden halt in the early 1950s. For the next 20 years, no improvement was seen in the death rate, a major indices of overall health, despite the fact that many of the miracle cures of modern medicine occurred during this same time. We have seen open heart surgery, organ transplants, trauma centers, and many other dramatic new life-saving techniques and developments become common. Thus, it appeared that despite our continuing investment in illness identification, treatment, and cure, we were seeing, for the first time, no significant improvement in over-all health. It seemed we had reached a point of diminishing returns on our investment.

An additional contribution to a changing view of health has come from findings obtained through epidemiological studies. Primary among them was the Framingham study—a longitudinal study that continues today in

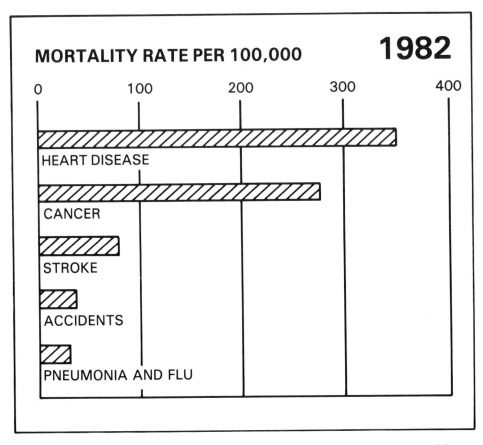

Figure 1.2. Mortality Data from National Center for Health Statistics: *Health, United States.* Public Health Service, 1983.

a small community in Massachusetts. Results from these studies identified four major contributors to early death and disease. They are:

1. Heredity
2. Environment
3. Medical care
4. Lifestyle

The accompanying pie chart (Figure 1.4) graphically illustrates the contributing proportion of each of these four factors to early death and disease. Clearly lifestyle, the way in which individuals behave on a day-to-day basis, is by far the most important factor affecting health and longevity. Yet most of us continue to rely on the physician to fix us when something goes wrong. Though our physicians and other health care professionals have an important role to play, they cannot be expected to take full responsibility for our health. Most physicians have had little, if any, training in such important health-enhancing disciplines as fitness, nutrition, and stress management, nor in methods to teach people new skills.

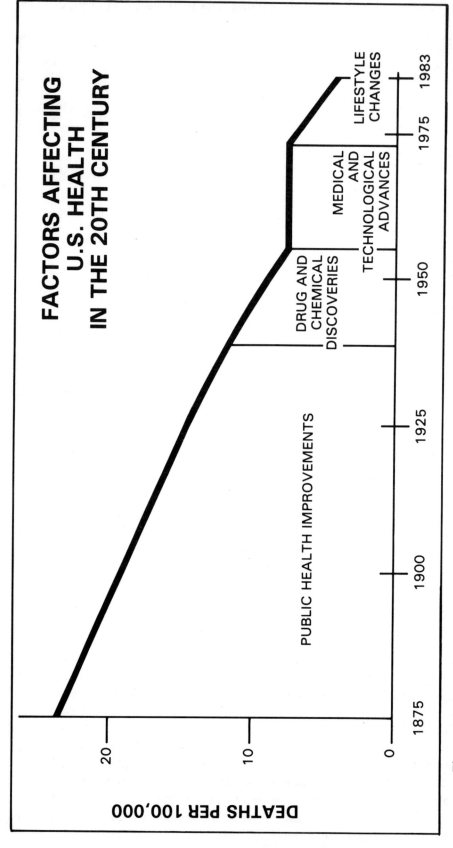

Figure 1.3. Mortality Data from National Center for Health Statistics: *Health, United States.* Public Health Service, 1983.

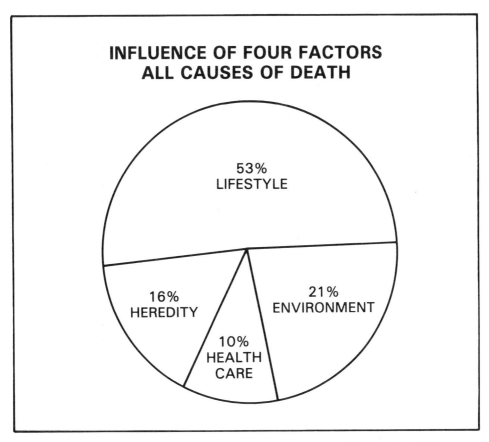

**INFLUENCE OF FOUR FACTORS
ALL CAUSES OF DEATH**

53%
LIFESTYLE

16%
HEREDITY

10%
HEALTH
CARE

21%
ENVIRONMENT

Figure 1.4. *From* Centers for Disease Control, Public Health Service, 1975.

Wellness and Health Promotion Defined

Many terms have been applied to the newly emerging concept of and approach to individual health and well-being. Wellness, a term first coined by Dunn (1960), has become the most prevalent of these. Other terms include lifestyle improvement and health enhancement. Wellness can be defined as <u>the</u> <u>process</u> <u>of</u> <u>adapting</u> <u>patterns</u> <u>of</u> <u>behavior</u> <u>that</u> <u>lead</u> <u>to</u> <u>improved</u> <u>health</u> <u>and</u> <u>heightened</u> <u>life</u> <u>satisfaction.</u>

Health promotion is the term most often used (as in the case of this book) when referring to the application of wellness principles to institutions and organizations. Health promotion, as a special case of the wellness concept, can be usefully defined as <u>the</u> <u>systematic</u> <u>efforts</u> <u>by</u> <u>an</u> <u>orga-</u> <u>nization</u> <u>to</u> <u>enhance</u> <u>the</u> <u>wellness</u> <u>of</u> <u>its</u> <u>members</u> <u>through</u> <u>education,</u> <u>behavior</u> <u>change,</u> <u>and</u> <u>cultural</u> <u>support.</u> Implicit in these two definitions is the idea that everybody, regardless of current health condition, is capable of making significant improvements in the quality of his or her life. Wellness, therefore, is not a landmark to be achieved but rather a continual process involving all components of one's life that impact on well-being.

Wellness is much more than mere physical health. Various models have been put forth to emphasize this multidimensionality. The Institute has adapted a model incorporating six dimensions. They are social, occupational, spiritual, physical, intellectual, and emotional. Numerous examples exist that highlight the strong interdependence of these dimensions in determining individual health. For instance, the relationships among emotional well-being, job satisfaction, and physical health have been well-established.

Each dimension is an opportunity for personal growth. For many, the physical dimension, incorporating fitness and nutrition, has been a rewarding way to engage in health-enhancing behaviors. For others, it may be the emotional dimension with its focus on stress management, relaxation, interpersonal relationships, and the like, that provides the greatest reward. Each dimension is an open door to opportunities in the others and success in one may support and fuel interest in others.

A useful paradigm for drawing distinctions between the traditional medical model of health care and the new conception of wellness is the wellness continuum first created by John Travis and further refined by other authors (see Figure 1.5). The middle of the continuum represents the absence of any discernable illness or disease. Most of us, if asked what our current state of health is, would answer "healthy" assuming we had no signs or symptoms of disease. Traditional medicine only becomes involved in our health by bringing its tremendous technology to bear on the treatment of "the problem" once it has occurred. The best that the medical approach can do is return us to the center of the continuum where there is no discernable illness. Health and wellness are, however, not simply the lack of disease. Rather, as the continuum illustrates, wellness is the active process of taking responsibility for our health through education, motivation, risk reduction, behavior change, and creating an improved quality of life. Dunn calls this "high-level wellness."

The Influence of Culture

We live in an illness culture. As Americans, we are constantly influenced by our family, peers, workplace, religious and community institutions, the mass media, industry, and our government to behave in ways that are detrimental to the quality and length of our lives. A powerful current of cultural norms shapes and directs our daily behavior. As children, we are rewarded with sugar for behaving positively; as adults, we are encouraged to consume food and alcohol in excess. Together with our over-reliance on doctors, drugs, and hospitals, the influence of powerful, subtle, and pervasive cultural norms has resulted in unnecessary, debilitating disease and premature death.

The effects of our culture can be seen in the success rates of typical health education programs. In the cases of smoking cessation and weight

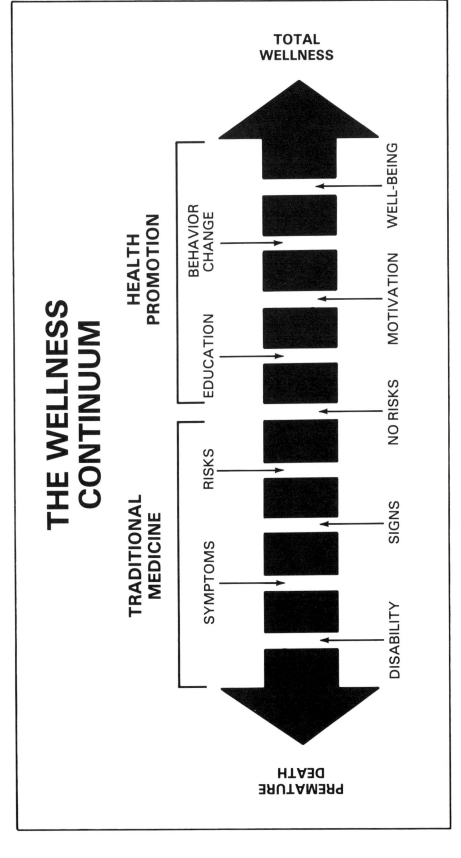

Figure 1.5. Adapted from the Illness/Wellness Continuum. Used with permission. Copyright 1972, 1981, John W. Travis, M.D. *From* Wellness Workbook, Ryan & Travis, Ten Speed Press, 1981.

reduction programs, a relatively high percentage of participants are able to successfully reduce weight or quit smoking but are unable to maintain the desired changes permanently. Long-term success rates for these and most behavior change programs are dismally low. Maintaining newly acquired skills has proven to be most formidable. Maintenance of positive lifestyle choices is best achieved when desired behaviors are supported and encouraged by the organizations and environment surrounding the person involved. If such support was generally provided, there would be little need for behavior change programs in the first place.

The health promotion movement is characterized by two major themes. The first is the importance of individual responsibility for one's health. This idea is based on the fact that the major determinants of health and well-being are factors over which individuals have a great deal of control. Therefore, it is inappropriate to delegate total responsibility for those factors to others such as the physician and psychologist. The second theme is the influence of cultural norms on individual choice. These two characteristics are, on the surface, contradictory. On the one hand, health promoters admonish individuals to take the responsibility for creating their own well-being, and on the other suggest that in large measure the way in which individuals choose to behave is determined by cultural influences beyond their immediate control.

This apparent contradiction can be at least partially resolved by adopting the former but recognizing the impact of the latter. Since the individual must accept and suffer the consequences of lifestyle choices, it ultimately rests on his or her shoulders to take responsibility for the results. However, the ease or difficulty of bearing that responsibility will be affected by the support, or lack thereof, given by the surrounding culture. It is important to understand that both characteristics have significant impact on the health promotion field.

Business and Health

Corporate America was the first major institution to adopt the wellness philosophy and implement health promotion programs for American workers. Industry incentive to do this is high. The cost of employee illness care is skyrocketing. Business and industry are paying one-third of the total medical bill for the nation. As organizations, employers are in a unique position to impact on the health of a large proportion of the American public. As individuals, we spend more time at work than in any other activity. Thus, it's not surprising that our work environment can have considerable influence, both positive and negative, on our health.

In many cases, organizations have a rather negative impact on their members. Figure 1.6 is an adaptation of the wellness continuum (shown in Figure 1.5) to the organizational setting. The Organizational Wellness

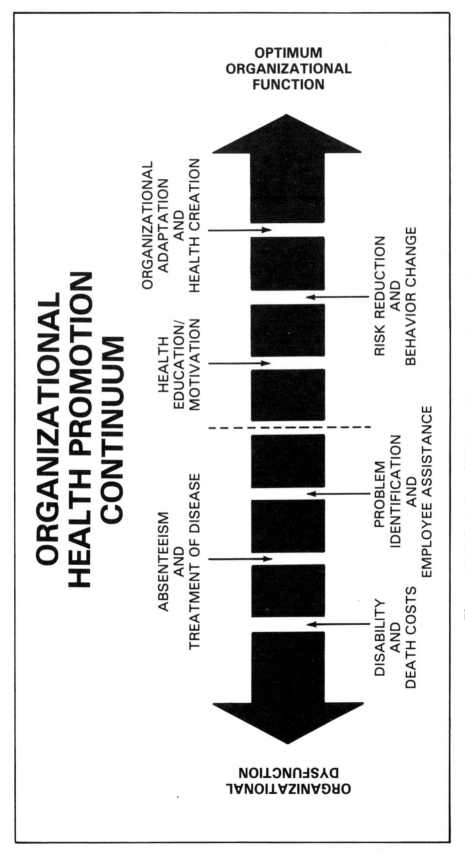

Figure 1.6 (Adaptation of Wellness Continuum shown in Figure 1.5).

11

Continuum illustrates how organizations can create environments conducive to optimal functioning or, conversely, to organizational dysfunction.

Many organizations continue to be reactive with respect to the health of their members. Such organizations are represented to the left on the Organizational Wellness Continuum. In this case, some basic programs or services may be offered to respond to problems as they occur. Examples include traditional health care insurance, disability coverage, and employee assistance programs. To the right on the continuum are organizations which not only meet these basic needs but go further by encouraging and supporting healthier lifestyle choices and, ultimately, creating an organizational climate which is healthy and alive.

Of course, business and industry are not the only sectors of our society beginning to actively pursue wellness from an organizational perspective. Colleges and universities, school districts, government, and hospitals are increasingly interested in encouraging a proactive approach to improved health. The wellness philosophy, and its application through health promotion programs and organizations, is in its infancy. However, its future growth and maturation is guaranteed not only because it makes sense but also because the alternatives no longer meet society's needs.

— 2 —

Organizational Involvement in Health

Organizations of all types, including business and industry, hospitals, schools and community groups, have adopted health promotion programs. But nowhere has there been more health promotion interest and activity than business and industry. Worksite programs designed to promote employee health have evolved for two reasons. First, most Americans will spend as much as one third of their adult lives at work. The worksite is an environment in which powerful incentives are offered, including wages and salaries, benefits, and social status. In addition, it is a place rich in social contact where behavior-influencing norms are established and maintained. Thus, it is an ideal place in which to provide individuals with opportunities and incentives for improving life skills. More than any other single institution, the worksite is a convenient and inexpensive location for programs which are easily accessible to large numbers of people in already established groupings.

The second reason the worksite is an ideal organizational setting for health promotion is that employers have strong incentive to encourage healthful behaviors among the organizational membership. The intolerably high and ever growing cost of providing health care coverage to employees is the prime reason for corporate health promotion. In addition, the health of employees affects productivity, absenteeism, turnover, morale, and even the image of the company and its ability to attract qualified personnel.

The Employment Relationship

Interest in promoting healthier employee lifestyles has not appeared suddenly but rather is a part of an evolutionary change in the way in which employers have dealt with the health of employees. This is part of a much larger, richer, and often turbulent history of the relationship between employer and employee.

The industrial revolution brought on a tidal wave of change in American society. The mass production of inexpensive goods was achieved with an unlimited supply of unskilled laborers eager to be employed at subsistence wages. The "human resource" was treated as an inexpensive, specialized piece of machinery which, when unable to keep pace with the other power machines in factory assembly lines, was discarded and replaced. Beginning as early as the 1700s and lasting well into this century, factory conditions were characterized by long hours, low pay, and dangerous work performed by anyone willing to do it—including children.

Labor Unions

The collective bargaining movement emerged in the late 1700s as a result of these intolerable working conditions. The first labor strike in America was by the Philadelphia journeymen printers in 1786. Though early court decisions placed substantial restrictions on the rights of workers to organize, the movement grew and labor organizations became a significant force in changing the work environment.

These changes, however, were not obtained without struggle and the relationship between laborers and their employers became increasingly strained. In the late 1800s violence among workers and management and civil authorities was frequent. During the civil war, the "Molly McGuires," Irish miners in Pennsylvania, committed violent acts against employers. In 1876, 10 of this secret society's leaders were executed, bringing the demise of the organization. In 1886, a strike for the eight-hour workday at the McCormick Reaper's Works in Chicago resulted in the deaths of 18 people.

It wasn't until the early twentieth century that the U.S. government, through congressional legislation, became involved in the relationship between employee and employer. Two significant pieces of legislation were the Clayton Act in 1914 and the Norris-LaGuardia Act in 1932. The Clayton Act exempted unions from the anti-monopoly provisions established by the Sherman Act. The Norris-LaGuardia Act protected labor unions from arbitrary injunctions against their activities. The labor movement was gaining acceptability.

Theories of Organizations

Paralleling the emergence of the industrial revolution and the collective bargaining movement was the development of scholarly activities concerning the organization. The first effort to understand and systematize the work process is attributed to Frederick W. Taylor. His "scientific management" principles became the accepted theory for efficient production in American industry. Taylor's work, which emphasized the simplification of tasks, included four basic principles of management:

1. Management could be a true science
2. Selection of workers could be improved through scientific processes
3. The worker could be educated to improve performance
4. Improved relationships between the workers and management would result in increased productivity.

The focal point of the scientific management movement was the use of time-motion studies which relied on the systematic observation of the specialized behaviors necessary for the worker to efficiently complete a task (French, 1978).

This rationalistic approach to improved productivity was carried to its extreme and continues to be emphasized in many management schools. In The Pursuit of Excellence (Peters and Waterman, 1983) the authors summarized this approach as an overemphasis on:

1. Big is better

2. Low-cost producers
3. Analysis of everything
4. Control and manipulation of all contingencies
5. Emphasis on incentives
6. Inspection
7. Ever increasing growth.

They summarize the limitations of this rational view as the inability to deal with informality, the lack of attention to values, and the lack of internal competition as incentive for improved productivity.

In 1923, an experiment conducted at the Western Electric Company's Hawthorne Works in Chicago resulted in unexpected findings which profoundly changed the prevailing theory of organizations. The results of an attempt to determine the effects of lighting on worker output proved to be paradoxical. Production went up when the lighting was improved, but it also went up when the lighting was severely reduced. This surprising result was attributed to the fact that the attention workers received from the experimenters seemed to improve their morale and motivation. The idea that psychological variables could affect production became known as the Hawthorne Effect. In large measure, this study was responsible for the emergence of the Human Relations Movement, which found social scientists concentrating on the impact of such psychological variables as leadership styles, motivation, and group cohesiveness on production output.

Social Legislation

Sweeping changes in the employment relationship occurred during the 1960s and 70s in response to major pieces of social legislation. The Civil Rights Act of 1964 restricted employers from discriminating with respect to employment practices (hiring, pay, promotion) on the basis of race, color, religion, sex, or national origin. The Act was amended in 1968 and 1972 and continues to have significant impact on the relationship between the worker and employer.

Further limitations were placed on the behavior of management as a result of the Vocational Rehabilitation Act of 1973 which required employers to promote opportunities for handicapped workers. Similarly, the Age Discrimination Act of 1967 protected workers from discriminatory employment practices on the basis of age.

The development of the collective bargaining movement, theories about how organizations behave, and the intervention of the courts and government in the employment field are necessary prerequisites to the development and role of health promotion. The establishment of a health promotion program requires an understanding of the historical, social, and psychological characteristics of the organization into which it is being introduced.

The Human Resource Management Process

Most organizational members are not likely to view their organization's health promotion effort as an overriding concern. For management, health promotion is embedded in a network of unrelated issues affecting the major goals of the organization, such as product markets, competition, government regulation, and production efficiencies. Even within the related area of human resource management, health promotion is but one of many issues affecting the employment relationship. For the employee, health promotion is most often viewed as a benefit received along with health insurance, pension plans, and other perquisites. These considerations ordinarily take the backseat to salary and wage issues, job satisfaction, and career advancement.

Personnel management is defined by French (1978) as the "recruitment, selection, development, utilization of and accommodation to human resources by organizations." To be effective, health promotion programs must be designed with an understanding of the structure and process of human resources management.

Corporation involvement in the health and well-being of employees is not new. As early as the turn of the century, a few companies had safety specialists and physicians whose task was to determine the suitability of the individual to the job. During the 20s and 30s, a number of companies created recreation programs for employees. In the 1930s, alcohol abuse programs were developed in response to a growing concern over the incidence of alcohol-related work problems. The realization that alcohol abuse precipitated, and was often hidden by, other problems affecting work resulted in the expansion of alcohol abuse programs into what are currently called Employee Assistance Programs or EAPs.

EAPs are typically a diagnosis and referral process available to all employees who have a concern about any personal problem affecting work performance. These might include financial difficulties, marital and family crises, or legal problems. Based on the results of the diagnosis, clients are referred to an appropriate community agency such as the family physician, a hospital, or another helping agency. The EAP is known as a broad bush approach to employee problems, with focus on reactive care rather than prevention or health promotion. The EAP concept has proved to be a valuable method of dealing with employee performance problems at the early stage of dysfunction. The employer, particularly the immediate supervisor, has a resource to turn to for assistance with the problem before drastic disciplinary action is required. Also, the supervisor is spared the need to intervene in the employee's personal affairs in order to correct the work problem.

The employee, through an EAP, has an unbiased listener to seek assistance from for any problem which affects performance. Most of the diagnoses made by EAP counselors continue to be related to alcohol or drug problems. The use of the broad bush approach has resulted in many employees seeking help for other problems (such as marital discord) when alcohol and drugs are the real cause of job performance decline.

In many occupations, the worksite posed, and in some cases continues to pose, a significant risk to the health and well-being of the individual worker. For this reason, the Occupational Health and Safety Administration (OSHA) was created by the federal government. Employers, through the encouragement of OSHA and on their own, have reduced the numbers of worksite accidents and occupational diseases through improved conditions and technology as well as health education programs. A notable example of the latter are efforts to train workers to avoid back injuries, a major work-related injury.

Despite the initiation of EAPs and safety and health education, industry has been unable to stem the tide of health care cost increases. Health promotion has become the new standard bearer in the battle to reduce costs, increase productivity, and improve the quality of work life. The growth of health promotion programs at the worksite is likely to continue as employers in all types of organizations—from small, privately held companies to large public agencies—realize the value (and cost) of their human resources and decide to maintain and enhance that resource.

— 3 —

Wellness as a Cost Containment Strategy

Although it has become cliché in wellness publications to highlight the financial resources being expended on health care in this country, these facts and figures have had the greatest impact on the growth and proliferation of health promotion programs.

To recount but a few of the facts:

1. In 1983, over 350 billion dollars were expended on health care. This represents 10-1/2 percent of the gross national product.
2. Over six percent of all American workers are engaged in health-related occupations.
3. We currently spend an average of $1500 per year on health care for every man, woman, and child in this country.

All of these figures are increasing. It is anticipated that by the year 2000 we will be spending one trillion dollars for our health care or $4000 per person. Of the 350+ billion dollars being spent annually for our health care, over one-fourth is subsidized by our nation's employers. It is, therefore, not surprising that the greatest interest in and impetus for organizational health promotion have come from the business community.

However, it is important to realize that there are many factors contributing to the escalating cost of health care. Health promotion is one of a number of efforts being made to reduce these expenses.

Health promotion requires long-term, gradual changes making cost benefit analysis difficult. Only in recent years have substantial data been accumulated indicating the potential cost savings organizations might gain from health enhancement activities. New models are now emerging to reduce health care costs, improve productivity, and encourage other positive organizational changes.

There are significant structural barriers to cost containment and reduction which are likely to be with us for the foreseeable future. An aging population with increased life expectancy, incentives which encourage the development and use of expensive equipment and facilities, and research which favors high technology illness care are all realities with which our society will continue to live for many years.

Current Issues Affecting Health Care Costs

Current theory underlying the wellness movement in this country espouses the following: As a nation, we are dying from very different diseases than we were at the turn of this century. Major causes of morbidity and mortality in the late 1800s and the early 1900s were primarily infectious diseases; factors contributing to these diseases were related to public health issues such as polluted water, inadequate water supplies, lack of sewage disposal, overcrowded housing, etc.

For most Americans, the serious consequences of such conditions (e.g., tuberculosis, pneumonia, diarrhea) have been eliminated and today the primary causes of death are what can be called "diseases of choice." Major killers are heart disease, cancer, stroke, and accidents. Factors contributing to each of these are, for the most part, factors over which we have some control such as smoking, lack of exercise, obesity, and nutrition. The health care community has responded to this dramatic shift in morbidity and mortality by continuing to treat the new diseases with traditional methods. That is, to identify symptoms and causes once the illness has occurred and then to seek its cure. Figure 3.1 illustrates the continued investment in traditional medical care.

This approach has proven to be less effective with new diseases than it was with old. For example, if we use the death rate per 100,000 as a good indices of the overall effectiveness of the health care delivery system, we find that the death rate stopped its steady decline about 1952 and remained unchanged through a period of time in which medical technology, miracle cures, and health care facilities were greatly expanded. (See Figure 1.3 in Chapter 1.)

It appears that we had reached a point of diminishing returns from investment in traditional, medical institutions. In response, came a growth of interest in wellness and health promotion based on the assumption that it is cheaper to prevent disease than to cure it. Many health care professionals believe that changing lifestyle and behavior are the most important strategies to improved health. Until recently, however, there has been little documented evidence to show that wellness programs in the business or organizational setting have produced the expected cost savings. This is not too surprising given that the primary benefit to lifestyle change is reduced risk of degenerative diseases which occur over long periods of time, sometimes as long as 20 to 30 years.

Treatment of illness rather than prevention is but one variable contributing to escalating health care costs. For individuals whose primary responsibility is health promotion, it is increasingly important to become interested in and familiar with other critical variables affecting the health of employees.

One such variable is the health care payment system. This system encourages unnecessary procedures, duplication of facilities and equipment, and unnecessary use of services. Health insurance plans afforded most American workers allow the insured employee to select his or her own provider. Given the choice, an individual often chooses the most expensive facility with the greatest number of services: the costs for these services are then paid by the third party insurance company who, in turn, bills the employer. In order to attract clients, hospitals, clinics, and physicians are encouraged to provide the most expensive and best services possible.

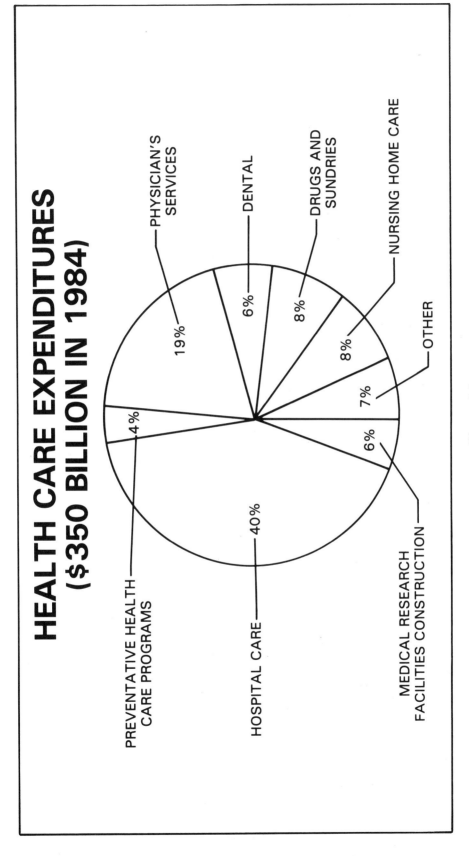

HEALTH CARE EXPENDITURES ($350 BILLION IN 1984)

PHYSICIAN'S SERVICES

DENTAL

DRUGS AND SUNDRIES

NURSING HOME CARE

OTHER

19%

6%

8%

8%

7%

4%

40%

6%

PREVENTATIVE HEALTH CARE PROGRAMS

HOSPITAL CARE

MEDICAL RESEARCH FACILITIES CONSTRUCTION

Figure 3.1

25

The costs assigned to particular services and procedures are not constrained by the principles of supply-and-demand. The current situation is one in which the demand for services is decreasing while supply of services is increasing. Yet, because the consumer of these services does not pay for them, there is every incentive for health care providers to increase prices. For example, the hospital with an increasing number of empty beds need only increase the cost per bed per day to offset reduced revenue resulting from fewer clients.

Pricing is not the only contributor to rising costs. The method of practice by physicians is changing as well. The number and intensity of services per patient are on the increase. There is some question about whether this change has any effect on improved medical care. Disturbing signs indicate that the trend of increasing costs is not likely to abate soon. For instance, there is a trend for physicians to join group practices rather than practice alone. According to the New England Journal of Medicine (Epstein, et al., 1983) physicians participating in large group practices order more tests at higher costs than do their colleagues in small group or solo practices.

Even more disturbing, and of much greater and more long-term impact, is the continuing trend in basic medical research towards expensive high technology equipment and procedures directed at acute disease identification and care. These new technologies, encouraged by a system which lacks cost controls, are likely to become the standard procedures of the future.

Finally, there is a trend towards for-profit hospitals and clinics in this country. Such corporate conglomerates now account for 40 billion dollars in annual gross revenues. These corporate giants must be responsible to shareholders interested in a fair return on their investment.

Strategies for Change

There has been a flurry of experimental programs developed by both small and large employers throughout the country in response to the 20 to 30 percent annual increase in health care outlays.

For many employers, the first step is to address the costs associated with the administration of employee benefits package. Two examples of efforts to do this include claims control and coordination of benefits. Claims control is an attempt to assure that health care charges are limited to those costs incurred by employees for which they are responsible. Coordination of benefits is designed to reduce multiple coverage (and, therefore, multiple costs) to the same individual. These and other administrative belt-tightening procedures have been successful; however, administrative costs seldom account for more than 10 percent of the total health care bill.

The real problem lies with the health care providers and their consumers. Walter McClure (1983) identifies two different types of incentive programs to reduce costs. The first, consumer incentives, encourages employees to reduce the cost of their health care. These would include incentives to stay healthy, to be judicious about choices of health care services, and to select more efficient providers. Bonuses for healthy lifestyles, deductibles for service usage, and selection of Preferred Provider Organizations (PPOs) and Health Maintenance Organizations (HMOs) are examples of these consumer incentive programs.

McClure, however, points out that programs to reduce employee use of services have limited cost savings because they frequently are services which cost less than $1,000. Expensive procedures, those costing more than $1,000, comprise the bulk (78 percent) of medical claims. Thus, it is the second type of programs, provider incentives, which will effect the greatest cost savings in the immediate future. Examples of provider incentives include programs with a maximum payout for each service, prospective payment rates, and utilization review.

Robert Murphy (1984) provides a useful paradigm for understanding the effectiveness of health-related cost containment programs by evaluating them on the basis of whether they will have immediate-, middle-, or long-range impact. The immediate-range programs result in savings immediately and typically include the administrative cost containment and utilization review programs previously mentioned. However, the effectiveness of some cost containment strategies is not realized for at least a year. These are the middle range programs. They include systematic planning efforts, regulation and resource allocation decisions, competition and consumer choice mechanisms, and efforts to promote voluntary change by providers. Murphy and others, have concluded that health promotions, as a cost containment effort, fall in the long range category. It may require five to ten or more years before significant, tangible financial benefits are realized from health promotion and health protection programs. However, the potential savings will be greatest from these long-range programs than from the short to middle range efforts.

Cost-Benefit Data to Support Health Promotion

An evolution in the sophistication and objectivity of the data to support health promotion programs is underway. Information supporting the effectiveness of health promotion and wellness programs can be categorized into three types.

The first type, and least objective, is the opinion survey, showing support for programs in terms of their effects on morale, absenteeism, and behavior change. In the early stages of most programs, this is often the best information available. But perceptions of change as the result of a program are of limited usefulness. An example of this type of information is provided in the Johnson and Johnson "Live for Life" health program. Participating employees estimated a 13 percent reduction in sick days while nonparticipants indicated a 9 percent increase in sick days taken (Savvy, December 1983).

The second type of information is data actually indicating a reduction in risk. This category represents the state of the art with respect to most established wellness programs. A more objective study using a quasi experimental design is underway at Johnson and Johnson (C. L. Murphy, 1983). The study will provide hard, physiological data to demonstrate the impact of the corporate health promotion program at selected sites. New York Telephone evaluated the results of its nine health promotion, disease-prevention projects and found a reduction in the risk factors of smoking, cholesterol, hypertension, and fitness (Berry, 1981). The underlying assumption which has received substantial support is that risk factors are directly and positively correlated with costs. Based on their findings, New York Telephone estimated the savings gained from the reduction in risks achieved. After subtracting the cost for conducting the programs, they showed a gain of $2,700,000 annually.

The third and most desirable type of data is information that shows a clear association between the health promotion program and cost savings in health care, disability and insurance premiums. This information falls in Murphy's long-range category of cost effectiveness. It is difficult to find more than a few examples of this type of information since most programs have not been in existence long enough for adequate information on savings to be obtained. However, in the few cases where information is available, the trend is very positive and encouraging.

The Control Data Experience

The Control Data Corporation has engaged in one of the most sophisticated and thorough studies to determine the impact of a health promotion program on health care and other costs. The program, called Staywell, was begun in 1979. Because the company's health insurance program is self-insured, and more importantly self-administered, the company is in the enviable position of having complete data on health care use. This allows correlations to be made between health promotion efforts and health care expenditures.

Impetus for program implementation was obtained from data which showed significant difference in costs between employees who were at greater risk of degenerative diseases and those who were not. Investigators found that employees who smoked, never exercised, were overweight, or were hypertensive, were more costly to the company than their lower risk counterparts. Also, similar relationships were found between health habits and absenteeism and work limitations due to illness.

The Staywell program was initiated in 1979 and focused on the chronic degenerative diseases, particularly cardiovascular disease and lung cancer, and their associated risk factors. The program, as of 1983, serves 22,000 employees and their spouses in 14 U.S. cities. Individuals pay nothing to participate in the program.

The occurrence of a degenerative disease is typically 20 or more years after the onset of a related risk factor. Thus, the impact of Staywell in terms of health cost savings is anticipated to take a long time. However, preliminary data, in the form of participant perceptions, suggests that individuals are changing behavior as a result of their involvement in specific behavior change programs.

At Contral Data, the computer is playing an increasingly important role in health promotion management. In other areas of cost containment, sophisticated models are being developed which also require the assistance of computer technology. One new and exciting area is in the application of the Health Risk Appraisal Systems to cost/benefit analysis of health promotion programs. A program manager, armed with group profiles detailing employee health risks can, for instance, estimate the number of heart attacks and lung cancers expected in the next 10 years if there is no intervention and can also estimate the savings which can, hypothetically, be obtained through risk reduction programs. Data such as this would provide powerful support for health promotion programming.

Goetz and Bernstein (1984) detail a method for collection and use of health risk data as a strategy to project savings from selected risk reduction programs. They caution that the maximum saving will be obtained when such programs are targeted only to high-risk employees rather than made available to all organizational members.

The Financial Dilemma

For many organizations, the cost of employee health benefits has grown to such proportions that the very existence of the organization is in jeopardy. In these circumstances, it becomes difficult for the organization to plan strategies which include health promotion and risk reduction components when the benefits of such programs are not likely to be realized for many years. Yet, the absence of health promoting efforts in employee benefits programs will, by default, place the organization on a path which will bring ever increasing health care expenditures. This creates a paradox for many organizations. On the one hand, they are in no financial position to initiate new programs from which they cannot expect relatively rapid results, and, on the other hand, they risk permanently escalating costs without the initiation of such programs.

The solution to this dilemma may be to take some of the savings obtained through short-range cost savings measures and invest them in

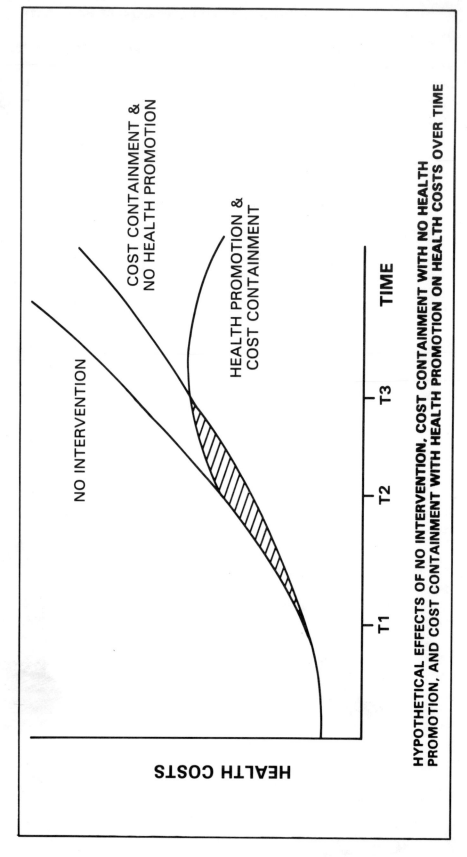

HYPOTHETICAL EFFECTS OF NO INTERVENTION, COST CONTAINMENT WITH NO HEALTH PROMOTION, AND COST CONTAINMENT WITH HEALTH PROMOTION ON HEALTH COSTS OVER TIME

Figure 3.2

health promotion and risk reduction programs. In this way, the organization foregoes some of the immediate gains of cost containment efforts in order to obtain long-term, permanent, and broader-based successes. Dick Huset (1983) hypothesizes that organizations which seek only short-term cost containment savings, and fail to invest some of those savings in long-range programs such as wellness, will find themselves on a gradient of escalating health care costs equal to that preceeding the cost containment effort. Only through reinvestment in long-range strategies will the cost containment curve abate. The accompanying graph (Figure 3.2) illustrates this idea. The shaded area represents the period of time from the onset of a health promotion program (T1) to the point where the program begins to save money (T2).

This discussion has centered almost exclusively on the financial savings to be obtained from various wellness and other types of health programs. It should be remembered that there are other important, but less tangible, economic effects to be realized from programs designed to improve the quality and quantity of employees' lives. The important variables of increased well-being, improved work attitude, team building and organizational morale, and positive family relationships must be taken into account. While no direct savings can be attributed to these intangibles, there is little doubt that they have a positive impact, financially and otherwise.

Conclusion

The only alternative to wellness programs which emphasize behavior change and cultural adaptation is continued escalation of the cost of health care. The current system is so ensconced (for-profit hospitals, medical schools, increasing illness identification technology) that the only long-term solution is to keep people away from it and thereby reduce its size and importance. Because decisions to invest in long-term changes in employee health have been delayed, the decision to make such efforts has become very difficult for many organizations. However, as data supporting the investment in wellness continue to be accumulated, organizations will begin to see cultural and behavioral change within their organizations as a high priority.

— 4 —

Health Promotion Planning

The Health Promotion Program Process

A great variation in approaches to program development exists from one organization to the next. It would be presumptuous to proscribe specific strategies for all organizations given their diversity. That no simple formula exists which will fit the needs of all or even most organizations should come as no surprise when one considers differences in size, mission (profit vs. non-profit and governmental vs. private), geographical location, available local resources, and the nature of the work force (white collar office workers vs. blue collar industrial laborers).

Despite this diversity, there are broadly defined stages which lend themselves to approaching this complex process in a systematic manner. Most organizations will need to address each to at least some degree. The accompanying diagram (Figure 4.1) lists the four major stages of the health promotion process and the order in which they occur. They are:

- Planning
- Assessment
- Implementation
- Evaluation.

The model, as an illustrative tool, is an oversimplification of the actual complexity of the process. All of the stages, once begun, are continuous processes throughout the life of the program. But, initially, it is important to first commit to the planning and assessment phases before attempting to begin actual programs.

Figure 4.1

During the planning stage, the organization defines its commitment and assesses its needs so that the course chosen for the program matches long-term goals.

During the assessment stage, information about individuals and the organization, which can be used to determine specific program needs, is collected. In addition, the assessment process itself is an intervention which has positive change implications.

During the implementation stage changes in behavior are attempted. There are three important components to the implementation stage. They are:

1. Education/Motivation
2. Behavioral Change
3. Organizational Adaptation.

Finally, during the evaluation stage, feedback necessary for assessing the program and determining its future direction is sought. Outcomes of specific programs and activities are evaluated.

Some have suggested that the only way to achieve a successful cost-saving, comprehensive, health promotion program is to purchase services entirely from large, outside service companies whose business it is to provide complete health promotion programs to organizations (Chadwick, 1982).

This approach neglects the tremendous internal resources of organizations which can, at little cost, be directed towards improved employee health. Most organizations have related programs, such as safety education, employee assistance programs, and training and development classes. These and many other similar internal resources, if forgotten in the development of a new health promotion program, would diminish the overall quality and ultimate success of the health promotion process. In addition, many individuals at all organizational levels have skills and expertise that can be tapped. Aerobic class leaders, former smokers, runners, and practitioners of yoga, stress reduction, healthy cooking, etc., are just a few of the "experts" available within most organizations.

Duff and Fritz (1984) support the need to develop programs tailored to each organization. In their discussion of stress management programs for organizations, they say ". . . it is important to keep in mind that no single stress intervention will be exactly right for all organizations, any more than a single treatment will be right for all individuals suffering negative stress effects."

Healthy organizations define their purpose with respect to widely accepted values. These shared values uniquely define the culture of the organization. When explicitly promoted and supported by the organization, they provide a powerful driving force toward organizational goal achievement (Peters and Waterman, 1983). It is philosophically inconsistent to attempt to apply health promotion programs which have been purchased as a complete package, without first carefully considering if they match the values, strengths, and needs of the organization. Such simplistic and "easy" answers to creating a healthier work force are doomed to fail.

However, there are individual components of larger "packaged" programs which may be appropriate within widely varying contexts. These components, such as health risk appraisals, weight reduction protocols, health education courses, and smoking cessation programs, are available from many sources which do not require the purchase of a larger package. As the health promotion and wellness field matures, community networks of health-promoting professionals will develop. The sharing of resources between corporations and community organizations will enhance the efforts of the individual organization.

Planning for Health Promotion Programs

Planning, the first stage in the health promotion program process, is an opportunity for an organization to establish long-range goals and objectives. In addition, the context and format to achieve these goals and objectives can be determined at this stage. The decision to establish a health promotion program might be based on specific problems or needs identified by the organizational leadership. These problems and needs become the framework for the planning process. Through systematic planning, clearly understood and mutually agreed upon goals are derived which, in the process, may result in a reassessment of the originally perceived problems and needs.

There are a number of important tasks which are required for the planning process to be successfully completed. They are:

1. Organizational Commitment. Initiators of the program need to define the parameters of the organization's commitment. Parameters which will limit the scope of the intended program may include the financial resources available for the program. Most organizations are unwilling to commit substantial resources to a program prior to the planning phase. More likely, seed money may be made available which will be used for the initial planning assessment stages. Expanded financial obligation can then be sought in conjunction with acceptance of a formal program plan. The amount and number of personnel committed to the project will determine the speed with which the program can be initiated. A program meant to become an integral and important part of the human resource operation will likely require the commitment of at least one full-time professional staff person.

2. Create A Formal Mechanism For Planning And Decision Making. In order to obtain the broadest interest in and commitment to a health promotion effort, some form of planning committee needs to be formally established and endorsed by management. The process of membership selection can take many forms, including appointment by departments and volunteers, depending upon where the initial interest in such a health promotion program is being generated. Committee members might be appointed by departments, or they might be chosen from volunteers. Programs initiated by upper level management will likely have a committee structure considerably different than those initiated within a specific department. Also, those taking part in the program planning

process are likely to influence the direction of the program based upon their previous experiences and organizational position. Thus, selection based on these factors can be pivotal to program direction.

3. <u>Establishment Of A Long-Term Mission And Goals.</u> Too often, expectations are not met because goals have been established which are unattainable in the short run. A three to five year plan is a reasonable time frame to achieve at least some organizational change. Intermediate goals (one to three years) can also be established. The long range goals are based on a definition of current problems and desired conditions. Johnson and Johnson Corporation established two primary goals in their Live for Life program begun in early 1979: 1) to provide the means for Johnson and Johnson employees to become among the healthiest employees in the world; and 2) to determine the degree to which the program is cost effective (Johnson and Johnson, 1983). Based on these broadly defined goals, program objectives were formulated and directed at improvements in nutrition, weight control, stress management, fitness, smoking cessation, and health knowledge. Other organizations may decide to concentrate their efforts in different areas. Some will focus on risk identification and reduction, others on fitness, fitness facilities, and the like. In any case, each organization must determine the mission of its program with respect to its own needs. Finally, the mission statement and goals should be formally documented and approved by management. This document thus becomes the cornerstone upon which all future programs and activities will be built and against which they will be judged. This does not mean, however, that the document is cast in stone. It should be flexible because as the program unfolds, new understandings of the organizational need will be gained. Adaptations can be made regularly which will maintain the document as an up-to-date program guide.

4. <u>Evaluation Design.</u> Using previously established program goals as a basis, it is necessary, during the planning stage, to decide (at least in outline form) what information must be acquired to evaluate the effectiveness of the program. This needs to be done at an early stage so that the tools and procedures used in the evaluation are a direct extension of the program mission and goals.

5. <u>Establish A Program Timetable.</u> An outline of the schedule of activities to be accomplished by the program managers should be formulated. This timetable will likely undergo regular revision, however, it serves as a guide for progress towards the long-range goals. The outline should include the estimated times for completion of the planning, assessment, and evaluation stages. The implementation stage timetable can only be determined after the completion of the assessment stage.

Planning Committees

The use of planning committees is the most prevalent mechanism for program development and implementation in the health promotion field. The ultimate success of a health promotion program will, to a great extent, be determined by the interest, commitment, and support of a wide cross section of the organizational membership. For this reason, the committee process, if employed, requires special attention. To be effective, a committee must have a mandate from the organization. Committees with little decision making power will fail to engender a commitment to the program from members and those they represent.

Careful consideration should be given to the makeup of the committee. Many possibilities might be considered when a committee is being selected; only a few will be mentioned here. Certainly, it would be important for members to have some expertise. Often, it can be useful to have as the committee chair the professional responsible for program implementation. In addition, most organizations have others with some expertise, such as corporate physicians and nurses, benefits administrators, and risk managers. The committee should also represent the broadest cross section of the organization and take into consideration career classifications (laborers, clerical, middle managers, and leadership), location, and departments. In addition, it is useful to include those who will be required to implement the program once it has been designed.

Finally, there is a point of diminishing returns in terms of the effectiveness of group decision making when the committee becomes too large and unwieldy. An optimum balance must be struck between adequate representation and size.

Decisions made by committee are not always as effective as those made by an individual administrator with substantial expertise. The overriding reason for their use, however, is that they are a consensus-building mechanism which can lead to broad based program acceptance. There are a number of factors which can affect superior group decision making. First, it is important that the group agree on its goals. In many cases, goals have, at least in broad terms, been established for them. Attempting to diagnose problems and establish solutions to those problems without first agreeing on the committee's goals will lead to contradictory decision making. The committee chair needs to discriminate facts from opinions and to focus attention squarely on the tasks at hand. One of the most beneficial outcomes of the committee process is the generation of a wide variety of possible program options and courses of action. The difficulty arises when it is necessary to select from among the many possible options that course of action which is best suited to the organization. Often, in an effort to reach consensus, the best solutions are neglected or watered down.

The members of a health promotion planning committee are the key to communicating interest and generating enthusiasm for the program. However, the planning process can be a long and arduous task. The interest and motivation of committee members must be maintained. There are incentives which the organization can use to maintain this enthusiasm. Time off from work for committee duties, special social gatherings for the group, outside visitations to other programs, and experimentation with assessments and tests that may eventually be used on the at-large organizational membership are examples of techniques to motivate committee members.

Adequate attention to the planning of health promotion programs can help organizations avoid unnecessary expenditures of limited resources on activities unrelated to important program goals. Through careful development of long range goals, the positive impact of health promotion can be realized and its worth can be accurately assessed.

— 5 —

Assessing Individual and Organizational Health

The Issues

Assessing the health of individuals and using the information collected can be complicated and time consuming. Assessments providing health information to individuals are by far the most prevalent activities of health promotion programs in the organizational setting. The emphasis on assessments is due primarily to the perceived educational and motivational impact of the assessment process. Assessment, whether it be a health risk appraisal, fitness test, blood pressure screening, or wellness inventory, has become the significant intervention mode of the organizational health promotion program.

It should be understood that the assessment process is the second of a four stage process. The assessment stage will follow the planning stage and precede the implementation and evaluation stages. In addition to their impact on the knowledge and motivation level of the individual, assessments provide important information to the health promotion program manager which will be useful for program design.

There are three key components to the successful implementation of a wellness program. They are:

1. Education and motivation
2. Behavioral change
3. Organizational adaptation.

The impact of individual assessments is most often focused on the first of these, the educational and motivational aspects. Unfortunately, many program providers limit their programs, and therefore the impact of such programs, to this first component. It is imperative, when designing programs, that consideration be given to the behavior change and organizational adaptation components as well. The greatest impact will be achieved by providing opportunities to change behavior as a result of knowledge and motivation gained through the assessment process. Also, effecting behavioral change is greatly enhanced by improvements to the organizational environment and culture.

There are three important reasons for the organization to provide assessments to individual members as a part of the organizational wellness process. First, and most important, is the positive impact that information about one's health can have on individual education and motivation for change. It is most difficult to make decisions about change without information about the need for change.

Second, information obtained through the assessment process about the relative well being of an organization's membership is useful in selecting appropriate programs and the format for those programs. Also, assessments can identify groups (such as individuals with a high risk of heart disease) to whom specific programs can be targeted.

Third, assessments and the information gained from them at the inception of a program are useful baseline data. This data can be used to evaluate the effectiveness of programs and services offered to improve the health and well-being of the organization's membership.

Health Risk Appraisals

The health risk appraisal (HRA) has become the most widely used method of assessment and intervention in health promotion programs. The HRA comes in many forms. In its most basic form, it is a standardized instrument which identifies individual risk factors by age, race, and sex. The risk factors are then used to project mortality (i.e., the likely life expectancy of the individual) based on national norms. The field of health risk analysis is by no means an exact science. Results will likely vary from one questionnaire to another since different organizations designing these instruments are including different questions with different assigned risk weights. The issue of accurate results from HRAs is important, but it must be realized that these instruments are not intended to predict future individual health. They are estimates of probability based on the health of others who answer in similar ways.

The use of these appraisals can be a powerful and inexpensive method of initiating a new health promotion program. Large numbers of people can be introduced to the concepts of wellness and prevention with information that is specific to the individual. In addition, the organization can take advantage of the information collected by summarizing the data to determine the overall health, as well as some of the specific risk factors, of its membership. This information can be used to target programs to specific groups as well as make estimates of the cost savings to be gained from health program interventions.

There are, however, a number of disadvantages with respect to the HRA that must be understood. First, the health risk appraisal, in and of itself, is a rather negative process and contradictory to a positive wellness philosophy. In its most basic form, it is an estimate of the respondent's likely age of death and the diseases which will most likely contribute to death. For this reason, a number of the available HRAs include sections providing information on aspects of an individual's health other than morbidity and mortality estimates.

One important component often included is a wellness inventory section. Wellness, as it is usually defined, includes all of the aspects of our lives—occupational, emotional, social, spiritual, physical, and intellectual. Wellness inventories are designed to provide some feedback on each of these important categories. The appraisal is unable to provide this information because no prospective or epidemiological data is available which can predict risk of disease or death for such variables as stress, occupational wellness, and even fitness. Wellness inventories, therefore, provide an opportunity to give positive and encouraging information to individuals about their lifestyle on a number of variables over which they have the greatest control.

Moreover, many of the risks identified in a standard HRA that contribute to a lowered life expectancy are risks over which the individual has little or no control. These sometimes include a family history of certain diseases, such as cancer, and the number of miles driven annually in an automobile.

The data used to build a health risk profile is complex, and, therefore, results can often be misinterpreted. One area often misinterpreted is the estimate of health age versus actual age. These estimates are based on answers which predict risks to the individual per 100,000 people of the same age, race, and sex (i.e., number of deaths per 100,000 people). Since the mortality curve rises with age, an increase in risk for an individual at one age can result in a very different increase in health age than for a similar increase in risk for an individual of another age. The chart shown in Figure 5.1 demonstrates this effect.

Using Health Risk Appraisals Appropriately

The following is a list of guidelines and recommendations for using health risk appraisals.

1) The instrument chosen should include wellness inventories and other positive information.
2) Confidentiality of results for individuals must be maintained. Information about the procedures which will be used to assure this confidentiality should be provided to individual participants.
3) Where appropriate, summary data describing the total group of participants should be available.
4) Group interpretations (sessions at which a number of people receive their results) are the best method for helping participants understand their results. If this is not possible, some procedure must be provided whereby individuals can obtain answers to questions about their results. Also, on occasion there are inaccurate results due to poorly completed answer sheets or computer error. Procedures to correct these errors should be provided.
5) The health risk appraisal and wellness inventory are just one part of a larger program. Since the health risk appraisal can be a motivational and educational tool, it is necessary that opportunities be provided to assist the individual in making the desired behavioral changes. Weight reduction, fitness, stress management, breast self-exams, career programs and the like, are examples of opportunities to link education to results obtained on the HRA.

The science of health risk estimation will continue to improve as more sophisticated and accurate data are collected on the health and longevity

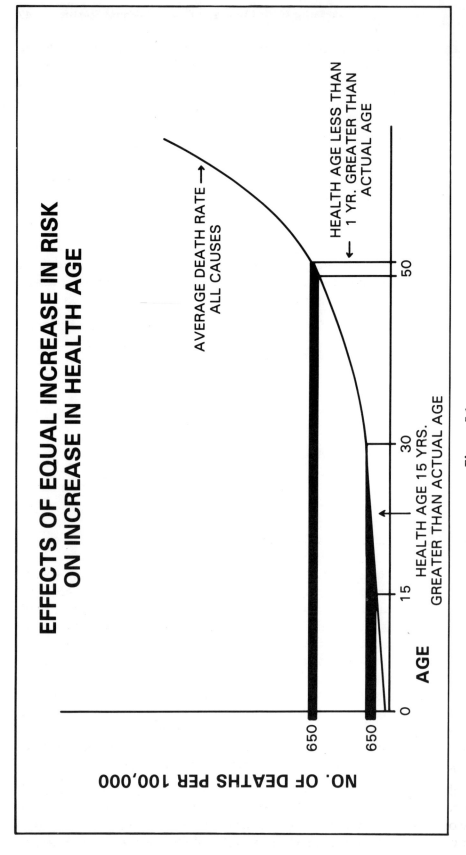

Figure 5.1

of the U.S. population and as our capacity to measure wellness grows. However, the practical use of these instruments in the organizational setting will remain somewhat limited unless the results are used to establish behavior change programs for individuals, make cultural change decisions for organizations, and investigate the relationship between individual risks and health care costs. (An example of a Health Risk Appraisal appears in Appendix A.)

Wellness Inventories

A popular and educational adjunct to the standard health risk appraisal is the wellness inventory—a list of questions which help the individual identify his or her strengths or weaknesses on dimensions of health not directly related to epidemiologic data and therefore not covered through HRA.

Wellness inventories typically solicit responses to questions in such areas as fitness, job satisfaction, nutrition, social support, and stress. Scores derived from completing the questions are usually an indices of the relative "well-being" of the individual when compared to an average obtained for a larger population (such as all company employees or all individuals having completed the questionnaire) on each of the dimensions. In some cases, results are reported using an arbitrary scale such as "doing very well" to "could make improvements." The benefit of the wellness inventory is in its educational value. It is a relatively simple, economic, and interesting method to learn about lifestyle habits and their impact on health. (An example of a Wellness Inventory appears in Appendix B.)

Interest and Need Surveys

Health risk appraisals and wellness inventories can provide the organization with information about the current health status of its membership. However, organizations must be concerned with the level of interest their members have in the program and also the needs of their members to satisfy those interests. Interest and need surveys can be useful in dealing with these concerns and can take many forms. For large organizations, it can be easiest to survey only a sample of the total population and make inferences from those results. Also, all of the information desired need not be collected at once. Since health risk appraisals and interest and needs surveys are motivational and educational interventions, they should be used on a regular and ongoing basis. The information collected can be used to change current programs and establish new goals.

Unlike the standardized health risk appraisal, needs and interest surveys can be tailor-made to fit the context of the specific organization. The type of work force, centralization of the work force, hours of operation, and many other variables will affect the design and implementation of a health promotion program. Survey questions should be written for the particular setting in which the program will be implemented.

Listed below are 10 general information categories that can be considered when designing interest and needs surveys. Within each category numerous questions could be included. It should be noted that it would be cumbersome and unnecessary to try to include questions from all of the areas in a single survey. The first four types are examples of information typically collected. The remaining six categories are examples of indicators of personal or cultural factors that can facilitate or inhibit lifestyle change.

1. Demographic Information. Age, length of service, job classification, type of health insurance coverage, and marital status are examples of demographic information which can be useful in determining the interests and needs of the surveyed population.

2. Health Habits and Condition. Interests expressed in surveys may depend to a great extent on the current health habits of the respondent. Health habits of interest might be whether the individual smokes, is overweight, exercises, or has high blood pressure. If the interest survey is accompanied by a health risk appraisal, care should be taken to avoid duplication of questions.

3. Program Interests and Preferences. This section of the survey is the most important in determining direction for programs. Information can be obtained here on the types of programs individuals might participate in, what their willingness is to pay part or all of the expenses for the programs, what times of day they are most likely to participate, and what length is most desirable for programs.

4. Knowledge of the Wellness Lifestyle. Questions which identify the knowledge level of employees about wellness can be both educational and useful in determining the level at which programs should be geared. Basic health questions might include knowledge of resting pulse, blood pressure, adaptive coping mechanisms, and nutrition.

(The remaining six categories are indicative of efforts to encourage grass-roots program acceptance and support).

5. Special Skills. In order to be consistent with the overall philosophy of encouraging participation by all members in a health promotion program, it is important that the interest survey reflect this philosophy. The survey is an ideal opportunity to solicit interest from respondents regarding any special skills, interests, or abilities that they would be willing to bring and share with fellow employees.

6. Worksite Conditions and Climate. The cultural milieu in which people spend most of their time will have much greater impact on behaviors affecting their health than will any single program or activity designed to directly change behavior. The interest survey is a good opportunity to identify work conditions or organiza-

tional policies (explicit or otherwise) that promote or inhibit good health. Examples of these types of conditions and policies are smoking policies, air quality in the work area, sick pay/well pay, food services, vending policies, stress levels created by over-crowding, dominating supervision, or lack of adequate incentives.

7. Program Management. Eventual program success will be sustained as a result of commitment to the program from a wide cross section of the organizational membership. This commitment will only be encouraged if the program is perceived to be owned by the employees themselves. The interest survey can encourage this sense of ownership by soliciting respondents to become involved in the design of the program and in its ongoing management. This may take the form of a planning committee.

8. Role of the Organization. The organization must be sensitive to the perceptions of its members regarding the appropriateness of the organization's intervention into individual health. In organizations where employee/employer relations have, historically, been strained, the involvement of the organization in employee health may be perceived as invasive. The answers to questions which identify these concerns will be useful in designing programs which give special care and attention to the involvement of employees in process.

9. Peer Group Leaders. Rank and file members are in the best positions to identify potential leaders for the health program. Asking them to recommend individuals who have special skills or who provide positive role models can help establish a strong base for program support as well as engender a sense of ownership among employees.

10. Cultural Pressure. Useful information can be obtained by asking respondents for their opinions about the organization's commitment to the health of its members. It's perhaps even more important to ask their opinions about the behavior of their peer groups—the people with whom they are involved during the work day. It can be an uphill battle for an individual who has decided to make significant behavior change to do so in the face of pressure by peers to do otherwise. The extent to which individuals perceive that they will receive support for positive behavior change from the corporation, the environment, coworkers, friends, and family can be useful data for program design. Also, information about the degree to which the individual is willing to support changes being made by others can serve similar purposes.

Questionnaire Design and Data Analysis

The design of a good questionnaire and the analysis of its results requires some knowledge of survey design and statistics. For the individual who is doing a survey for the first time, it will be helpful to seek the assistance of someone with some experience in an effort of this kind. Results obtained from poorly written questions or surveys with low participation rates will be of limited use and will hurt the credibility of the program. The following are some technical guidelines to be considered in survey design and data analysis.

1. Before writing any questions, clearly define the purpose of the questionnaire. What, precisely, do you want to learn from the results and in what form do you want the results? For instance, use of objective, forced-choice responses (such as true/false or strongly agree/strongly disagree) may be the easiest to tabulate and interpret; however, you must decide whether these responses will give you the information you need. Will you lose important information by not allowing subjective, open-ended responses?

2. What are the costs for obtaining the desired information?

3. What will be the acceptable response rate, and how will you assure that this response rate is obtained?

4. Who will use the questionnaire findings? Will the information be used by management for budget purposes, or will it be used by employees to assist in the design of programs? Those who are involved with the use of the data should be involved in questionnaire design.

5. What will be the reading level of the respondents?

6. Each question should be clear and unambiguous.

7. Keep questions as short as possible.

8. Eliminate any bias from the question. Sometimes questions can reveal the perspective of the questioner. Response options should be consistent. For example, to the question, "How often do you exercise?" the following response options would be inappropriate—never, rarely, weekly, monthly. A more appropriate set of response options might be—never, rarely, seldom, sometimes, often, or less than monthly, monthly, weekly, daily.

9. Response options should be exhaustive and should not overlap.

10. The questionnaire should provide clear instructions about how it is to be completed and where results are to be sent.

11. Careful consideration should be given to the length of the survey. The longer the survey, the lower the response rate and the less accurate responses will be.

Two useful references for the design of questionnaires are Bouchard (1976) and Smith (1975).

Comprehensive Multiphasic Health Screening

A recent trend in assessment of physical health has been the growth of organizations selling multiphasic screening services, particularly to employer organizations. Typically these services include the screening of all interested employees on a comprehensive battery of physiological tests including EKGs, X-Rays, urinalyses, and complete blood workups. Organizations enter into a contract for either a flat or per-employee fee with the testing organization. Mobile units run by technicians, rather than physicians, are often used to provide the services on site. On the surface, the notion behind this new service appears to be wise and prudent. That is, through early detection, symptoms and diseases which otherwise would have gone unnoticed are caught early, thereby allowing an individual to avoid the exorbitant cost of disease treatment.

However, growing evidence suggests that these tests are not cost effective and, in fact, may create more problems than they alleviate. Many of the tests and services provided through multiphasic screening are often free to many employees who are members of HMOs. In addition, for those organizations contracting for a flat fee, the usage rate tends to be very low and, therefore, the per-person cost is exorbitant.

Although some of the tests, such as measurement of cholesterol level, blood pressure, and hearing, are useful, it also appears that many of the tests are unnecessary. Other screening devices, such as the EKG and chest x-ray have been rated as money wasters or required only under special circumstances. The American Cancer Society has recommended that the chest x-ray should be discontinued for detection of cancer. According to the Harvard Medical School Health Letter (July, 1980), "Almost any test or exam will occasionally uncover an important abnormality. Careful study indicates that the cost (or even the risk) of many traditional procedures far outweighs the rare benefit derived when they are done routinely on a healthy person." The Letter has this to say about some of the specific tests administered in typical multiphasic screening programs: Blood counts and urinalysis—blood tests, checking for anemias, and a urinalysis checking for kidney and bladder ailments and diabetes—need be run only every three to five years. Multiple blood screening tests—to help diagnose specific problems, and to measure cholesterol, blood sugar, blood urea nitrogen, and calcium levels—should be conducted only once every five years. Though an EKG at age 35 will give a baseline pattern for an individual that can be used to detect subsequent deviations, the Letter says, "Annual cardiograms in the absence of chest pain make more dollars than sense."

The belief that giving as many tests as possible, since the vein is punctured anyway and the additional tests are therefore cheaper, is erroneous. There are a few measurements that have value, such as height, weight, blood pressure, and cholesterol/HDL. These tests can predict with some accuracy the probability of a healthy person becoming ill. Any additional tests add little to the predictive, but they do cost time and money and generate false positives which must be checked by a physician.

The conclusion one reaches on review of evaluations of multiphasic screening programs is that:

1. Many of the tests and their results are expensive and unnecessary when performed on normal and healthy individuals
2. Many of the tests that are useful should be targeted to specific individuals for whom the results can be most beneficial
3. The findings often create false positives (results suggesting that a problem exists when none does but requiring a physician to follow up to verify the findings).

Tests used selectively with high risk groups are a more legitimate and less expensive method for early detection. Allocation of scarce resources towards long-term behavioral change programs to improve employee lifestyles is likely to have a more meaningful impact on health care costs than most of the information obtainable through multiphasic screening programs.

Evaluating Outside Vendors

The assessment process may show a program need for which there are no resources inside the organization. It then becomes necessary to select an appropriate vendor to provide the desired program or service. Such programs include fitness facilities, health risk appraisal systems, and introductory wellness presentations.

In some cases, all that is required is the guidance or program formats available from outside individuals or organizations. Examples of this type of outside support are the American Lung Association's "stop smoking" program and the American Cancer Society's breast self-exam program. Though the protocol and training are provided by the outside organization (at no cost in the case of the two preceding examples), the actual intervention is accomplished internally.

Selecting a vendor is not as easy as it may seem. Many factors must be evaluated in the decision-making process. The following are the most important.

1. Competence. Insist on references from other organizations with whom the vendor has worked. Experience should show the adequacy of the product or service for use with a similar population in a similar environment.
2. Price. In many cases, information, program protocols, and advice can be obtained for free. When costs are involved, bids should be obtained from the vendors determined to be competent. When only one vendor appears to fit program needs, negotiating for a price lower than their first offer is certainly appropriate. Selection based on price may involve consideration of partial or full payment by program participants. This is no reason for concern and, in fact, may be desirable. Supporting the cost of a program when that cost is fair and reasonable and the program is professionally done

engenders a commitment on the part of the participants which can contribute to program success.

3. <u>Availability.</u> Programs provided by outside vendors must meet the special needs of the organization and not those of the vendor. The time of day, sessions per week, length of sessions, and location of programs need to be established with the best interests of the organization in mind. The vendor may be a valuable resource in determining what will work best.

Once the desired vendor has been selected, a contract or letter of agreement needs to be completed which clearly spells out the responsibilities of both parties. It may be useful to include in the agreement provisions for an evaluation of the program or services, and options to repeat or continue it in the future.

Conclusion

Under the best of circumstances, with carefully designed instruments and high participation rates, the results of an assessment program may still be ambiguous and contradictory. Yet the process is clearly a necessary one leading to heightened program interest, improved program outcomes, and a richer understanding of the organization and its impact on individuals. Ultimately, periodic assessments can have a positive cumulative impact on the organization's effectiveness in reaching its goals.

— 6 —

Program
Implementation

The third, and most important, stage in the development of a comprehensive wellness program is the implementation stage. As discussed, long-range program goals and objectives are established in the planning phase. The needs and interests of the organization's members and the resources and commitment of the organization to the program are considerd in this stage. Following the establishment of clearly defined objectives and long-range goals comes the task of assessing both the organization and its members to determine what specific activities are likely to get the program off to a successful start and what the formats for those activities should be. Thus, the actual implementation phase of the program should only occur after a great deal of groundwork has been completed.

The implementation of programs, encompasses the specific activities and options to be offered which are intended to improve the health and well-being of the organizational membership. They can be classified into three types:

1. Education/Motivation
2. Behavioral Change
3. Organizational Adaptation.

Each is integral to the successful implementation of a comprehensive health promotion program.

Education/Motivation Programs

For most employees in an organization initiating health promotion programs, the program's concepts and ideas are new and not entirely understood. The first task of those establishing the program is to educate the membership about the importance of self-responsibility and lifestyle choices in determining personal health and well-being. Second, the individuals must be motivated to make new choices which affect their health. It may be that for many new programs, educating and motivating individuals are all that can be accomplished in the short-term. Health risk appraisals, wellness inventories, interest and needs surveys, and health fairs are all examples of programs designed simply to heighten the awareness of members about their health and the impact that they personally can have upon it. Especially powerful tools are those which provide direct and individualized feedback to the individual such as health risk appraisals, wellness inventories, fitness assessment programs, and blood pressure monitoring. An example of an effective program format for creating interest in wellness among a large segment of the population is the use of wellness orientation sessions. These programs are typically half-day affairs during which individuals are introduced to the concepts of wellness, self-responsibility, the impact of lifestyle, and the influence of the environment and culture on their behavior.

Following this general presentation, specific components of lifestyle change can be addressed, the most popular being nutrition and weight control, stress management, and fitness. The orientation session format provides an ideal opportunity to present an interpretation of previously completed assessments and to publicize upcoming behavior change programs.

Behavioral Change Programs

Once individuals have learned about their health, and the impact that they can have upon it, and are motivated to make changes in their lifestyle, opportunities must be made available for them to pursue these changes. Too often, organizations invest solely in educational programs, offering no effective options for individuals desiring to make changes. The impact of this short-sighted approach is occasionally seen with the use of health risk appraisals. The results of these assessments usually include a list of the individual's top 10 risks and recommendations on how to reduce those risks. With no follow up opportunities to make the recommended changes, the initial impact of the health risk assessment process is lost.

Behavior change programs are participatory activities in which the individual can learn new skills (such as relaxation techniques and exercise routines) or reduce or extinguish undesirable behaviors (such as smoking and overeating). Most programs are class-like in nature having an instructor, meetings once or twice a week, and groups of 30 or fewer. (Examples of behavior change programs appear in Table 6.1.)

A model program sponsored by the American Cancer Society (ACS) has the potential as a behavior change strategy far beyond the specific educational program to which it was originally intended. Breast cancer is the leading cause of cancer deaths among females in the United States. The ACS has made a special effort to educate women in early self-detection of precancerous lumps through breast self-examination (BSE) programs. In order to reach large numbers of women at the work site, a unique approach using a "health education network" was developed. The details of this strategy are worth considering not only for breast self-examination but also for the potential application of the model to other behavior change programs.

An organization, in agreeing to adopt the breast self-examination program, asks each of its department or unit directors to identify individuals (preferably women) to act as networkers. The ideal ratio is one networker for every 25–30 people. Individuals are chosen based on the following four criteria. They must have:

1. Good rapport with co-workers
2. An interest in health promotion programs
3. A willingness to participate
4. An ability to feel comfortable discussing the issue (in this case, breast self-examination).

Table 6.1   Types of Programs with Examples

Evaluation/Screening Programs	Behavior Change (Participatory Programs)
–Health Risk Appraisals	–Aerobic Exercise
–Wellness Inventories	–Running Clubs
–Breast Self-Exams	–Stress Management Training
–Fitness Evaluations	–Smoking Cessation
–Hypertension Screening	–Back Strengthening
–Multiphasic Screening	–Self-Care Skills
–Diet Analysis	–Blood Pressure and Pulse Monitoring
–Stress Evaluation	–Nutrition Modification
	–Weight Reduction
	–Career Evaluation and Goal Setting

Educational/Motivational Programs	Organizational Enhancement Programs
–Health Risk Appraisal Interpretations	–Healthy Foods Program
–Health/Wellness Fairs	–Air Quality
–Wellness Lectures	–Smoking Policies and Enforcement
–Back Education	–Personnel Policies (e.g., sick leave)
–Alcohol/Drug Awareness	–Professional Development
–Breast Self-Exam Education	–Worksite Stress Assessment
–Nutrition Education	–Employee Assistance Programs (EAPs)
–Fitness/Weight	

The networker is responsible for:

1. Attending a one-hour training session
2. Personally inviting each of her 25–30 co-workers to a BSE seminar
3. Registering interested women in available workshops.

All of their work is done on company time.

The second important phase of the health education network is the selection and training of <u>facilitators</u>. Facilitators are women willing to serve as instructors for the seminars. These women volunteers are required to learn BSE instruction, taught by physicians selected and provided by the American Cancer Society. Each facilitator agrees to teach four to six 30–40 minute seminars attended by 15–30 women. Facilitators' training and seminar instruction is on company time.

The American Cancer Society BSE program has been successfully implemented with a number of large employers including the Hennepin County work force in Minneapolis. Hennepin County, an employer of 8,000, initiated the BSE program in 1982 as part of its employee health promotion program called <u>WellWay.</u> The final program report (Tvedten, 1983) was revealing. Virtually every one of the 4,800 female employees received a personal invitation to and information about a seminar from a co-worker. As a result, over 2,200 (48 percent) women attended one of 137 seminars offered, and 86 percent of those who signed up actually attended a seminar. Evaluation results showed that, after the seminar, there was an increase in women's confidence in detecting lumps, knowledge of BSE procedures, and frequency of self-exams.

The health education network concept has important and far-reaching implications. The use of co-workers to market a program to the work force and to carry out the program with only limited outside direction has the potential for widespread application. Once an organization has completed the first program using the health education network concept, the networkers are then in place and can be called upon for future programs such as smoking cessation, blood pressure screening, and fitness testing. Reduced costs, worker ownership of health promotion programs, increased participation, and ultimately, improved individual and organizational health are all potential benefits of this powerful and progressive behavior change model.

Organizational Adaptation

For most wellness programs, the scope of their involvement is limited to activities within the previous two stages—Education/Motivation and Behavioral Change. Yet the third stage is perhaps the most significant because the most powerful influences on individual behaviors within an organization are most often the physical, social, and psychological environments. Subtle but pervasive norms are created in every organization which determine behavior and distinguish appropriate behavior from inappropriate behavior. Thus, organizations which hope to significantly improve the health of their members must account for the influence that the organization's culture has on the ability of individuals to choose new lifestyles. Sick leave policies, food choices, peer pressure, smoking policies, and even noise levels are all factors which can influence the quality of the working environment and ultimately individual health.

The following example is illustrative of the impact of organizational culture on a health promotion program. Obesity is often cited as a significant health risk to many individuals and a subject in which there is often a great deal of expressed interest. In most cases, employees who are overweight are familiar with the risks that they run and often express an interest in making lifestyle changes in order to reduce their weight. In addition, many are involved in company- or community-sponsored weight reduction programs. This might involve weekly or bi-weekly lunchtime sessions on weight control and visits to local for-profit weight clubs. But for many of these people (despite their knowledge level, motivation, and efforts to change eating behaviors), the major factor influencing their ability to lose weight is their home or work environment. Work breaks with peer groups continue to include sweet rolls and coffee; lunchrooms offer limited choices; and work schedules and the sedentary nature of some jobs provide little opportunity for exercise during the work day. It is no wonder, then, that the success rates for behavior change programs such as smoking cessation and weight reduction are miserably low.

Therefore, a significant and critical part of implementing health promotion in the organization is changing the culture in which individuals spend much of their time. A significant part of this change/effort should include strategies which influence individuals within their peer groups. This means involving all organizational members in the health promotion process, including the planning and designing of programs. The best way to change individual, long-term behavior is to create a positive, healthy, work site culture.

A Technology for Behavior Change

Successful change programs involving the extinction and replacement of undesirable, wellness-inhibiting behaviors with positive health-enhancing behaviors and skills, have incorporated in some measure the powerful technology of behavior modification. This technology is based on the principles of operant conditioning developed by the behaviorist, B.F. Skinner (1954). His scientific approach to human behavior has been most successfully and widely used with behavior disorders in controlled institutional settings. More recently, health promotion practitioners have identified behavior modification as an important tool for improving health education and promotion programs (Green and Stainbrook, 1982).

The most intractable problem for behavior change programs is not the actual change but the maintenance of desired change once it has been adopted. Becoming a non-smoker is much easier than staying a non-smoker and reducing weight is achieved with less struggle than maintaining a lower weight. Many of the contingencies which maintained the unwanted behavior in the past will continue to be present after the initial behavior change. The successful program takes this into account by helping the individual to understand the factors which elicit the undesirable responses. Once understood, the environments in which these factors occur (home, work, community, school, etc.) can be changed or avoided so desired behaviors can be practiced and rewarded. Ultimately, these desirable behaviors replace the undesirable ones.

It can be said that one person's reward (positive reinforcement) is another's punishment. This is so because most of our behavior is not controlled by primary reinforcers such as food, water, sex, warmth, and novelty but rather by factors which are associated with them. These associated factors, called secondary reinforcers, include most verbal and non-verbal communications (such as compliments and money). For some, cigarettes are associated with a primary reinforcer such as food and, thus, elicit a pleasant experience. For others, they are a noxious, adversive stimulus to be avoided. The contingencies which have shaped and continue to maintain undesirable health behaviors are complex. A smoker's desire to have a cigarette can be set off by hundreds of different environmental stimuli. In order to permanently break the unwanted habit, the factors which contribute to and reinforce the desire must be manipulated. Alternative environments which elicit and support the new, more desirable behavior must be found or created. Some of these environmental changes can be accomplished on an organizational or community-wide basis. Changing the food options in the company cafeteria and enforcing smoking policies are examples of organizational change which ultimately will be supported through consensus.

The application of behavior modification principles to health promotion programs is becoming more prevalent. Weight Watchers, Smoke Enders, biofeedback, and many other similarly successful approaches to behavior change rely to some extent on behavior modification. The following are the four important principles of behavior modification.

1. Positive Reinforcement. The immediate reward of a desirable (or for that matter any) behavior increases the likelihood of that behavior occurring again. In other words, a stimulus which has as its effect the increase in probability of occurrence of the immediately preceding behavior.

2. Negative Reinforcement. (The response-contingent removal of an aversive stimulus.) Negative reinforcement is often confused with punishment. However, punishment involves the presentation of an aversive stimulus in order to decrease the probability of a behavior, while negative reinforcement involves the removal of an aversive stimulus in order to increase the probability of a behavior. In effect, the removal of unpleasant conditions strengthens prior behavior. For example, absenteeism or avoidance of work will be reduced (i.e., more work behavior will be performed) when unpleasant, stressful work responsibilities and conditions are removed. In other words, when poor work conditions (aversive stimulus) are removed, there is an increase in the likelihood (reinforcement) of work behavior.

3. Extinction. When reinforcement is withheld, the results are a lower probability that the immediately preceding behavior will occur again. As an example of this principle, consider the smoker who lights a cigarette and is ignored by those to whom he or she is speaking. Assuming that the conversation was a desirable experience (positively reinforcing), the withdrawal of that stimulus as a result of the smoking behavior will, in principle, reduce the likelihood of the smoking behavior occurring in the future.

4. Punishment. The response-contingent application of an aversive stimulus immediately following a behavior which results in a decrease in the probability of a recurrence of that behavior. Using smoking as an example again, punishment might be the forced inhalation of noxious smoke by the smoker which pairs the cigarette smoking behavior with something extremely undesirable and reduces future smoking behavior.

These four basic principles have spawned an effective technology of behavior change which, in short, is based on the notion that through manipulation and control of the environment (including the human and organizational milieu) individual behaviors can be changed. Applications of these principles include behavior modeling, systematic desensitization, and contingency management.

For some, this idea of external control of the individual smacks of coercion. Such concern has limited the widespread application of this awesome technology. Yet, critics should realize that:

1. If not intentionally and systematically controlled, behavior is still controlled in part by the environment—better that it be based on rational choices than on random processes.
2. The individual determines the kind and degree of manipulation based on his or her own desire to change.

In this regard, "free will" is increased. The negative connotations associated with the terms behavior modification and behaviorism have encouraged the use of alternatives such as behavioral risk reduction, cognitive behavior therapy, and contingency management.

The impact of cultural influences on individual choice has been emphasized earlier (Chapter 1) as a key ingredient to defining the parameters of individual health choices. The technology of behavior modification is the application of principles of behavior change which grow from this cultural understanding.

Groups Norms

The reason individuals are so strongly influenced by group members is that groups control many of the stimuli to which the individual must attend. Cues given by peers provide the individual with subtle (and sometimes not so subtle) indications of the group's acceptance or disapproval of behavior. Behavior which gains approval is often rewarded. Rewards might come in the form of status symbols, monetary gain, or preferable assignments meted out by the group.

Another type of influence by groups is the stimuli which are provided simply by virtue of membership in a particular group. These stimuli are a normal part of the group environment, available to all group members, and can include stimuli in the work environment, interaction with group members, and other aspects of the work environment.

Hackman (1976) labels the former class of stimuli as, discretionary stimuli and the latter, as ambient stimuli. Discretionary stimuli are those which the group (and its individual members) have control over, and ambient stimuli are simply those which are present to all members and over which the group has no control. Hackman states further that ambient and discretionary stimuli can each influence individuals in three ways. The impact of a stimulus can result in:

1. Informational change (on member knowledge)
2. Affective change (on attitudes)
3. Behavioral change (behavior in the group).

Table 6.2 provides examples of the influences of ambient and discretionary stimuli on health behavior and shows distinctions between the two.

Group member influence on the behavior of an individual through manipulation of (discretionary) stimuli provides a normative based example of the affects of the technology of behavior modification. Groups have great control over the circumstances which elicit "appropriate" or "inappropriate" behavior as defined by the group. The task for those interested in effecting positive health change in groups is to encourage the group to reward healthy behavior exhibited by individual members. Also important are efforts to change the group environment (ambient stimuli) so that the group is not unnecessarily subjected to dangerous, stressful, or unpleasant working conditions.

Principles for Initial Programming Efforts

Every organization is unique. Health promotion strategies effective in one organization may not be effective in another. Each organization must take pains to determine its own needs and abilities to deliver health promotion programs. However, there are some general principles which can be useful guides for organizations:

1. Administrative Leadership and Support. It is important that from the outset, the leaders of the organization support the goals of the program and that this support is communicated to all organizational members.
2. Design Based on Needs and Interests of Membership. It may be that some programs will be offered which are of high interest to organization members but not directly related to specific program goals. However, by accommodating these interests, the long-term success of the program will be enhanced because the membership will have been given an opportunity to become involved in pro-

Table 6.2   Examples of Ambient and Discretionary Group Stimuli Influencing Health Behaviors

Ambient Stimuli	Affect on Health Behavior
(Based on group membership) Group status as attractive	
Other people	Opportunities for social interaction, friendship, lack of conflict, support
Tasks	Packing, difficulty of task, rest opportunities, exercise opportunities and facilities
Workplace conditions	Lighting, air quality
Discretionary Stimuli	
(Selectively administered by group members)	
Approval/disapproval	Support for food choices, clean air, etc.
Money and other rewards	
Models of appropriate behavior	Leader or supervisor engaged in healthy behaviors
Instructions of appropriate behavior	Rules, suggestions, and explicit goals for healthy behavior group

gramming decisions. This involvement can lead to other activities which may be more directly related to program goals. In addition, membership involvement in program determination will increase the sense of ownership for the programs on the part of the members.

3. Visibility. Special effort needs to be given to creating a highly visible program throughout the organization. It is through these initial marketing efforts that the program will establish itself as a credible and permanent organizational entity.

4. High Probability of Success. Programs which generate little or moderate interest, appeal to a very small segment of the organization, or require a great deal of credibility and trust, should not be attempted early on. Information obtained through the assessment process should indicate which activities are imminently doable and likely to succeed; these should be included in early pro-

grams. Programs on testicular self-exams and yoga may evoke interest from some and meet program goals, however, in most organizations, these would be risky ventures and better delayed until the program has achieved wide-spread organizational acceptance.

5. <u>Emphasize the Positive.</u> All too often, health promotion programs are limited to activities directed toward risk reduction. By definition, risk reduction has to do with avoidance of disease and early death—rather negative ideas. Though this may be a significant goal of the program, efforts to attain a reduction in risk must emphasize the positive aspects of lifestyle change. People are unlikely to make lasting lifestyle changes if the changes do not have some intrinsic rewards involving positive experiences. One suggestion for accomplishing this is to highlight the immediate short-term benefits in addition to the long-term impact of the changes made.

6. <u>Assure Access To All Organizational Members.</u> Very often programs are advertised as available to all, yet the design and format of the activities may make it difficult for some members to participate. Cost, times of day, and location can all be limiting factors for some members. It is also desirable, where possible, to encourage the involvement of family members. Clearly, behavior change efforts which are not supported and reinforced by an individual's family are much less likely to succeed.

7. <u>Evaluate Results.</u> Information obtained both during and after the completion of specific programs can be useful in modifying the activities more closely to meet the need of its participants and to design new activities.

The number of different program possibilities and the ways in which they can be implemented is almost endless. The most difficult task for many organizations will be to select from among the many possibilities those few programs that will best meet the needs of individuals and the goals of the organization.

— 7 —

Program Evaluation

Too often, evaluation of programs, products, and services is given only casual attention. Fundamentally, evaluation is the determination of the worth of something. Thus, accurate information describing the worth of health promotion programs and services is critical to making appropriate program choices and improving on those choices.

The evaluation process is antecedent to the planning, assessment, and implementation phases of the health promotion program. That is, to determine a program's value, the program must first be developed and implemented. Yet, for the evaluation to meet its intended goal, the design of the evaluation process must occur in the planning phase. Decisions about what is to be evaluated, who will be doing the evaluation, the manner in which the evaluation is to occur, and, finally, the uses for information obtained in the evaluation process need to be made prior to the assessment and implementation stages.

Roles of Evaluation

Michael Scriven (1973) suggests that in addition to the goal of evaluation, which is to assess program worth, there are two primary roles which evaluation can play. He calls these roles formative and summative evaluation.

Formative evaluation is the continuous and informal process of reassessing and improving ongoing program activities. By this definition, almost any health promotion professional is involved in formative program evaluation. The coordinator of a corporate health promotion program is frequently required to make decisions about such things as the time of day and length of programs, selection of program content, and methods of disseminating information. Decisions such as these are often the result of informal judgments based on recent programs' successes and failures.

Examples of formative evaluation measures include:

1. Numbers of programs offered
2. Numbers of participants
3. Opinions and other feedback from participants
4. Breadth of program topics
5. Feedback from group leaders and instructors.

The second and more important role of evaluation is the summative role. Summative evaluation is a more formal process than formative evaluation and is a systematic preplanned effort to obtain data and information useful in determining the effectiveness of completed programs.

There are two primary targets for summative evaluation. The first and more obvious is the assessment of specific program results to determine if they have achieved their intended objectives. For example, an objective for a weight reduction program might be that 50 percent of the participants achieve significant weight loss and maintain that weight loss for a period of six months. Program outcomes can be compared directly against the objective to determine program success.

A second target of the summative evaluation process is to determine the appropriateness of the goals and objectives of the program itself. Efforts to measure the effectiveness of the overall program and its long-range goals gets to the heart of the program's worth. Using an example similar to the one above, it might be asked, "Is the goal of weight reduction important? If so, is it more important than other programs that might otherwise have been provided?"

The following are examples of health promotion program goals amenable to summative evaluation measures.

1. Reduction in early death and disease
2. Reduction in risk factors (smoking, obesity, high blood pressure)
3. Changes in other health-related behaviors (emotional well-being, job satisfaction, alcohol and drug use)
4. Reduction in absenteeism
5. Reduction in health care and other benefits costs
6. Increase in knowledge about health and lifestyle factors affecting health
7. Enhanced organizational stature (community visibility, improved employee recruitment).

Figure 7.1 illustrates how formative and summative evaluations complete the health promotion program process.

Considerations in Designing Evaluation Studies

The task of program evaluation can be a difficult one particularly for individuals inexperienced in data collection, instrument design, and statistical analysis. For these and other reasons, it is often advisable for the program coordinator responsible for evaluating the success of the program to seek advice from and involvement of others from within or outside the organization to assist in the design and completion of the study. Though not all of the following are a requirement for every evaluation, they are useful guidelines for most situations.

Clarity	Is the purpose clearly understood and articulated prior to the onset of the evaluation process?
Validity	Does the study evaluate what was intended? How generalizable are the findings?
Reliability	Do the measurements used provide accurate information?

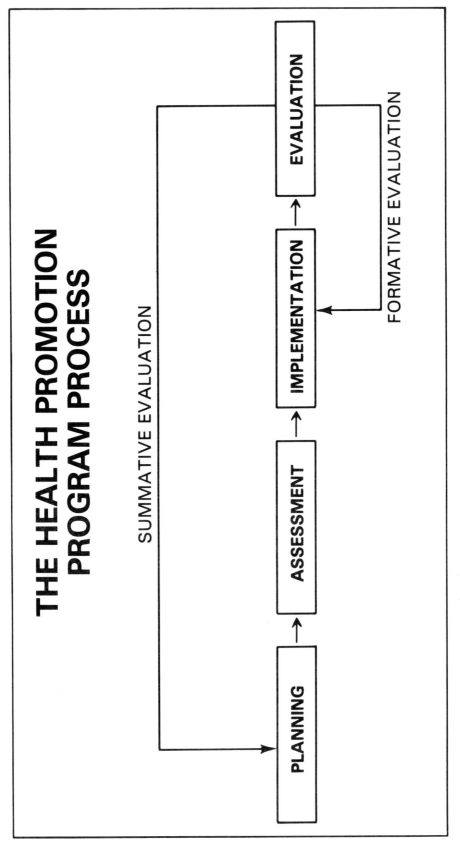

THE HEALTH PROMOTION
PROGRAM PROCESS

PLANNING → ASSESSMENT → IMPLEMENTATION → EVALUATION

SUMMATIVE EVALUATION

FORMATIVE EVALUATION

Figure 7.1

IMPLEMENTATION OF A COMPREHENSIVE ORGANIZATIONAL WELLNESS PROGRAM

	PHYSICAL FITNESS/ NUTRITION	SPIRITUAL	EMOTIONAL	SOCIAL	OCCUPATIONAL	INTELLECTUAL
EDUCATION/ MOTIVATION						
BEHAVIORAL CHANGE						
ORGANIZATIONAL ADAPTATION						

Figure 7.2

<u>Objectivity</u>	Are the interpretations of the findings consistent among multiple observers?
<u>Need</u>	Does the scope of the evaluation meet its intended need? Is it over- or under-designed?
<u>Credibility</u>	Will the outcome of the evaluation be used in making program decisions?
<u>Effectiveness</u>	Does the design meet the intended needs of the study? Are the findings targeted to the appropriate audience(s)?

The evaluation process can easily be forgotten among the many activities and responsibilities of a health promotion director in the midst of a growing and active health promotion program. Periodic, formal consideration of the impact and effectiveness of health promotion scheduled into the regular work calendar will help to avoid this problem. The accompanying figure (Figure 7.2) is a helpful guide for evaluating the depth and breadth of program activities. All past programs and efforts can be classified by the dimension of wellness and the stage of implementation into which they best fit. In this way, a picture emerges which suggests areas where much has been accomplished and areas which may still require attention.

— 8 —

Marketing Health Promotion

The successful achievement of health promotion program goals is necessarily linked to the effectiveness of efforts to obtain an acceptable level of participation by organizational members. Health promotion marketing is the set of strategies and activities systematically designed to communicate about, and direct the individuals toward, health promoting programs and services.

Conventional marketing wisdom holds that providers of products and services are engaged in marketing when they seek to meet the needs of the consumer. This definition, though partially true, fails to account for the fact that much of what marketing specialists do is designed to create new consumer needs. That is, they seek to influence the desires or needs of consumers so that they become interested in or ready for a product or service in which they previously had not been interested. Numerous examples of this type of marketing exist. For example, the tobacco industry engaged in a systematic marketing effort in the 1930s and the 1940s to get the female population to smoke. Prior to this time, it was socially unacceptable for women to smoke, i.e., it had not been a need.

Those involved in marketing health promotion must also be concerned with providing for the current needs of the consumers and changing the attitudes of those not yet convinced of the benefits of a healthier lifestyle. Marketing programs limited to the former will reach only those already convinced. Such "saving the saved" programs are a wonderful benefit for those who choose healthy lifestyles anyway but have little impact on the larger population to whom the programs must be directed if they are to achieve their long-range goals.

Don Ardell (1984) suggests that reaching those who are in the most need for wellness programs is one of the great challenges to the health promotional professional:

> "Too much current energies are spent . . . 'preaching to the choir' of true believers. . . How do we 'sell' wellness to the folks who crowd the sports stadia, the bars, the bowling alleys, and fast food emporiums? How do we 'win friends, and influence people' for wellness who watch daily soap operas, crowd the bingo parlors, and play video games?"

It is apparent that marketing our health promotion programs and activities is much more than simply distributing information specifying the time, place, and price of a particular health promoting activity.

Developing a marketing plan is an integral part of the health promotion planning process. The ability to reach a target audience can determine the type of program or service to be established. William Laser (1971) and other authors have suggested four basic strategies for consideration in the development of the marketing plan. They are known as the four P's—product, place, promotion, and price. The product strategy involves developing the right product for the targeted market. In health promotion, this means careful selection of programs based on an assessment of audience need. The place strategy is concerned with getting the right product to the marketplace. Here attention is given to where the target audience can obtain the desired products or services. The promotion strategy is concerned with communicating to the market audience the right product at the right place. This strategy most often comes to mind when one thinks of marketing and is exemplified by publicity, advertising, and selling. The price strategy focuses on determining the appropriate price to promote the product or service. It is often necessary in selecting health promotion programs to give thought to the resources of the organization and the willingness of participants to pay for part or all of the program. The application of the four P's to the marketing of a health promotion program is expanded upon below.

PRODUCT

1. Branding. The selection of a program name and logo is an important first step in obtaining program visibility and acceptance. Organizational members, once familiar with the program name and its identifying symbol, will more readily accept as credible the services and activities which are promoted under its banner. An identifiable name and logo also serve as a way to distinguish the program from other activities and services being promoted by outside organizations. Very careful consideration must be given to the overall program name and the titles of specific program activities. The name must be both descriptive of its purpose and positive in its image. What are the intended objectives of particular programs and what can the individual participating in these programs expect to achieve? Without being overly optimistic, the program planner, in conjunction with instructors or other providers, should be explicit about what participants can expect.

2. Features/Formats. Smoking cessation, weight reduction, stress management, and many other content areas can be applied in very different ways. Behavior modification, hypnosis, and group therapy are just three examples of the many methods which can be applied to a behavior change program such as smoking. Selection of the appropriate method will most likely be determined through the assessment process and trial and error. The selection of assessment tools and other devices or products used directly by organizational members should be based not only on their content but also on such considerations as the participant's reading level, social status, and age.

3. Fashion Cycles. Popular methods today may be replaced by new ones next year. The current popularity of aerobic dancing may be replaced by some new, and as yet unknown, aerobic exercise in the future. Thus, it is necessary to be sensitive to and prepared for changes of interest which will lead to new program formats.

PLACE

1. Integration. The mix of programs going on at any one time or place and the order in which they occur are two important considerations in the determination of program marketing. Many individuals can be introduced to and educated about lifestyle factors and from there, they can be directed to specific behavior change programs. The order in which these activities occur can encourage greater participation and sustained positive behavior change. Also, the provision of simultaneous programs may cause conflict for space, instructional time, and competition for participants.

2. Location. Access to the program can determine its success. Having a convenient location, whether it be at the work site or near home will obviously encourage greater participation. It is also important to consider what kind of facility is most desirable for the program. The need for privacy, shower facilities, quiet space, and air conditioning may be determined by the type of program initiated.

3. Time. Selection of the time of day, and day of week for programs will be determined by the particular audience desired. If a major program goal is to encourage participation by large numbers of individuals who are otherwise disinclined towards health promotion, then it may be desirable to obtain approval to use time to introduce the program and its activities. Once some initial interest has been aroused, activities scheduled before work, at lunch, on breaks, after working, and during evenings and weekends are all possible.

4. Length. Programs focusing on education and motivation are typically lecture-type programs lasting an hour or two or, at most, a half-day. On the other hand, behavior change programs, to be effective, must allow time for learning and practicing new skills. Typical course lengths for smoking cessation, weight reduction, stress management, and aerobic dancing classes are from six to sixteen weeks with sessions meeting two to four times a week.

5. Exposure. There are some programs which are not specific activities but, rather, are directed at changing the organizational environment. Programs of these kinds include the alteration of food service menus, poster campaigns, smoking policy enforcements, and blood pressure screening programs which are ongoing and long-term efforts. However, in initiating such change, some specified time period should be considered so that an evaluation of the impact of these efforts can be determined.

PROMOTION

1. Advertising/Publicity. Newsletters, flyers, posters, cafeteria table tents, brochures, and banners are just a few examples of many of the advertising tools that have been effective in promoting orga-

nizational health promotion programs. How to select the target audience and develop advertising materials to effectively reach that audience will be determined by knowledge of the location and context in which individuals will receive the information. Regular and repeated exposure to program announcements from more than a single advertising source can be expected to have greater impact than a single announcement from only one source.

2. Program Promotion. Program sessions themselves offer ideal opportunities to promote other organizational health promotion programs. Virtually every organization has meetings, seminars, training sessions, and social gatherings at which participation in the health promotion program can be encouraged.

3. Person To Person. One of the most powerful advertising tools is word of mouth. Knowing that one's fellow workers are participating in a new program will likely have much greater influence on an individual than impersonal advertising. This one-to-one contact can be formalized using a program of facilitators and peer group leaders. Such a program, sponsored by the American Cancer Society in its breast self-exam program, is discussed earlier (Chapter 6).

4. Cooperation. Since health promotion activities are occurring in many organizations and in most communities, there are great opportunities for joint efforts at both advertising and carrying out programs between and among neighboring organizations. Most communities have local groups such as YMCAs, recreation departments, public health departments, hospitals, clinics, and schools which frequently are sources of programs which can be advertised and shared with organization members. In many cases the publicity tools can be obtained free of charge.

PRICE

1. Introductory Pricing. Getting a new program off to a successful start may require that some initial activities be provided at no cost. As mentioned before, introducing the concepts of health promotion and motivating people to make choices for improved lifestyles ideally should be offered at no cost. Also, by using in-house personnel program costs to the organization can be minimized.

2. Shared Costs. There is great advantage in asking participants to pay at least some of the cost for behavior change programs because it encourages a commitment to program completion. For those participants lacking personal resolve to change behavior, a complete subsidization of the program by the organization will likely result in low success rates. The ideal pricing structure is one which is low enough to encourage adequate participation rates, yet high enough to assure program completion by most, if not all, of the participants. For most organizations, financial resources available to

health promotion programs are so limited that complete subsidization of participant programs is out of the question. However, some support by the organization can go a long way towards assuring its membership that it is committed to their improved well-being.

3. Budgets. Appropriation of monies towards health-enhancing activities must be given careful consideration. Though building fitness facilities is a desirable goal, the amount of money needed will necessarily not be available for other programs which may be of equal importance and which may, in the long run, have a more positive and widespread impact on the organization. In planning for future programs, cost will, to a great extent, determine how many programs and participants can be accommodated.

Professionals in the health promotion field have a great deal to learn from the marketing industry. Advertising directed at encouraging individuals to purchase products or engage in behaviors which are detrimental to their health is pervasive. A great deal can be learned from the advertising methods of the tobacco, food, and alcohol industries. To compete effectively with them, publicity for health promotion programs must be exciting, appealing, and impressive. At the same time, health promotion programs, and the publicity for them, must not only be giving consumers what they want but also encouraging them to make choices which are in the best interest of their long-term health. A balance must be maintained between giving individuals only what they perceive their needs to be and attempting to radically change their behavior with products and services ahead of acceptable social norms.

— 9 —

The Health Promotion Professional

There is at present no single formalized career path for those seeking to become health promotion professionals. The field is too young for such structured academic and experience-based programs. Individuals serving as health promotion professionals have come from widely varying backgrounds and areas of expertise. For most, the chosen career path was originally intended for a different occupation. Physicians, nurses, health educators, personnel and benefits administrators, public health officials, and physical education and recreation teachers have found their way into the health promotion field. Although still an emerging career field, some important skills and abilities can be identified as necessary for those who hope to function effectively in it. Perhaps at some point in the future, certification will be required for those who wish to enter careers in this field. Already, there are formalized undergraduate and graduate academic programs being established for the training of health and wellness professionals. (See Appendix C for a list of universities offering academic programs in health promotion.) However, even within higher education there is marked variation in the choice of which academic department will house such programs. Public health, psychology, and physical education are the three academic areas most often chosen to develop health promotion programs.

For most practitioners, expertise has been gained through self-instruction and personal experience. A frequent misconception is that managers, coordinators, and directors of health promotion programs necessarily need to be expert in most, if not all, of the common risk reduction programs such as smoking cessation, weight reduction, fitness, and stress management. More likely, program leaders will rely on others with expertise, or at least interest, to implement these specific program components. As the health promotion field matures, with increasing understanding of the process of individual and cultural change within organizations, the role of the health promotion professional grows increasingly more complex and demanding. As an example, the relationship of health promotion programs to other employee benefits is one which requires knowledge of governmental regulations, health maintenance organizations (HMOs) and preferred provider organizations (PPOs). The health promotion manager will undoubtedly be called upon to interact with many related organizational areas.

Roles of the Health Promotion Professional

The sophistication of the work force, complexity of the behavior change process, and impact of social and organizational factors on the work environment are contributing to the development of an increasingly responsible and ambiguous role for the managers of organizational health promotion. There are five broadly defined roles which characterize the activities of most successful program coordinators. They are the roles of leader, communicator, manager, role model, and facilitator.

1. <u>Leader.</u> The leadership style and ability of the director of a new health promotion program to effectively gain support, provide direction, and maintain enthusiasm for the program will, to a great extent, determine its eventual success. This is not to say that the sole responsibility for program maintenance is on the shoulders of the leader. French (1978) supports this contention in saying that, "Optimum effectiveness in leadership can take place only in an appropriate total organizational climate." He suggests that characteristics of subordinates and superiors and the goals of the program will affect leadership style.

2. <u>Communicator.</u> Writing reports, memos, letters, planning and evaluation documents, as well as speaking to groups, convincing decision-makers, and developing and disseminating information about programs to organizational members are activities regularly required of the health promotion professional.

3. <u>Manager.</u> Even the smallest programs will require the development of budgets, purchasing, contracting with vendors, marketing, and personnel supervision. Also, each of the four stages in the health promotion process (planning, assessment, implementation, and evaluation) require substantial knowledge in many areas. Skills needed can vary from the evaluation of appropriate assessment tools and program providers to evaluation design and to the collection, analysis, and interpretation of findings.

4. <u>Role Model.</u> It is hard to imagine an effective health promotion program led by a less than enthusiastic pursuer of a wellness lifestyle. This is not to suggest that the health promotion professional must be an exemplar of all that is characteristic of wellness. Rather, it should be obvious that the individual is making efforts towards improved well-being. The old adage, "Beware the adipose physician," applies equally well to individuals in health promotion.

5. <u>Facilitator.</u> Most programs developed to promote organizational health have focused on risk reduction activities. Individuals responsible for the development and management of these programs frequently spend their time as <u>programmers</u>—selecting, scheduling, and coordinating specific risk reduction programs. Though an emphasis on programming for risk reduction may be a legitimate activity for some organizations, particularly in the program's early stages, the programmer role denies the importance of participant input into the program process. The programmer, even with the best of intentions, becomes the sole determiner of the organization's health enhancement efforts, leaving little room for individual initiative and program ownership. Therefore, a more effective role is that of <u>facilitator</u>, one who assists organizational members to achieve their personal health goals.

Facilitating positive change, thus, requires both risk reduction expertise and greater enabling skills.

The Entrepreneur

The rapid growth in health promotion has spawned a major industry providing products and services, from fitness equipment to program consultants, to individuals and organizations. Many career opportunities are already available in this area. Rather than employees of organizations with responsibilities for managing in-house programs, many professionals will be engaged in developing new products and selling them to organizations.

A career in health promotion whether as an in-house program manager or as an independent entrepreneur, offers great potential for the innovative, self-directed individual. The prognosis for the future suggests rapid growth in virtually all organizational settings. A concomitant growth can therefore be expected in the numbers of competent professionals needed to create, develop and administer these programs.

— 10 —

Hospital-Based Health Promotion

Hospitals are experiencing changes as never before. Increased competition from health maintenance organizations, reduced demand for their traditional services, and increased pressure to hold down costs are forcing new organizational constraints. The hospital of the next century may resemble its current counterpart very little, and yet many hospitals have yet to respond to society's changing needs. When responses do occur, they are often reactive with little consideration for the long-term best interests of either the hospital or the community it serves.

But a new age in medicine is dawning and an increasing number of hospitals are attempting to meet the challenge head on. Health promotion has become a strategy for many hospitals to overcome the crises they now face. In 1981, the American Hospital Association (AHA) reported that 504 hospitals, or 9.3 percent of all AHA member hospitals, had some type of wellness or health promotion program (American Hospital Association, 1982).

There are compelling reasons for hospitals to enter the health promotion arena. A successful health promotion program can:

1. Reestablish the hospital as the center for health in the community
2. Increase revenues lost through reduced use of other services
3. Enhance its standing with the business and political community with respect to competing community hospitals
4. Generate increased business for other hospital services by bringing in new clientele
5. Improve the work environment of the hospital and the health of its employees.

Hospitals have always enjoyed a noncompetitive marketplace. When a person becomes ill, the physician prescribes a course of treatment which is paid for most often by the person's third party insurer, be it Medicare, Medicaid, or an employer's insurance company. Hospitals simply provide facilities and services roughly equal to the expected community demand for them. If their estimates are in error, the prices for the services are simply adjusted to account for the difference. Price does not affect demand.

Health promotion services, whether directed towards individuals or business and industry, involve free choice on the part of the purchasers. They can decide whether they want the service and from whom they will buy it. This situation is an unusual one for the hospital administrator. It requires new approaches with different skills and expertise, particularly in the areas of marketing and sales.

For the hospital, establishing the health promotion program can be difficult. Health promoting activities are in sharp contrast to the usual activities of a hospital whose primary focus has been disease identification and treatment and emergency care. A new program emphasizing health maintenance and enhancement with its reliance on education and behavior change is likely to be met with some resistance by hospital staff—particularly physicians.

Getting Started

In most hospitals where health promotion programs have been started, the importance of first establishing an internal program for employees has been recognized. The reasons for this are convincing. First, if the hospital is sold on the need for and the effectiveness of health promotion, then it is natural that, as a large employer with high health care costs, it would want to pursue that kind of program for its own employees. The hospital would gain the same benefits that any other employer would gain.

Second, internal activities to promote health will go a long way to convince individuals and organizations outside the hospital that it is committed to the health promotion concept. Hospital clients may be skeptical of the physician who attempts to convince them to enter a hospital-sponsored program if they see a disproportionate number of hospital staff who are overweight or smoking and if they are served food which is obviously less than nutritious.

Finally, an internal program is an ideal testing ground for services which are to be marketed to the community. Hospital employees may be the toughest customers to convince and, therefore, a useful audience for initial programming. Materials, instructors, and program protocols can be assessed for their acceptance and effectiveness before being subjected to the scrutiny of the marketplace.

Initiating a health promotion program with the intention of selling it to the community requires detailed planning and assessment. If the program is designed to be sold to business and industry, a careful study of the marketplace and the hospital's ability to respond to the needs of that marketplace must be done. Questions must be answered such as:

- Who are the potential buyers?
- How many employees do they have?
- What type of work do they engage in?
- Who else is offering health promotion services?
- What kind of services are they?

Careful market research using questionnaires, information from the Chamber of Commerce, and personal contacts will often reveal that some local companies are already prepared to initiate a health promoting activity. An assessment of the current health status of employees for the purpose of determining the need for a health promotion program and its potential benefits is often the first step taken by many organizations. Providing this assessment to an organization meets the immediate need of that organization and may also serve as a catalyst for further, more profitable cooperation between the hospital and the firm. Once established, this assessment program can be marketed to other corporations.

Before making the program fully operational, the following are points to be considered:

1. Organizational Structure. How will the program be organized, and what type of individuals will direct it? Most hospitals have incorporated the new program into an existing department. Others have created new entities with independent boards of directors. The good health program at the Skokie Valley Community Hospital in Skokie, Illinois is a good example of the latter. They have chosen to create a separate organization with its own board of directors and budget.

2. Funding. A realistic estimate of the start up costs is necessary. Is the program meant to break even, make a profit, or simply serve as a catalyst for other hospital business?

3. Pricing. Determining how much to charge individuals and corporate clients is not an easy task. Price can be based on a number of factors including the cost of providing the program, the competition, and need for revenue.

4. Program Design. Selecting specific programs, their content, and their format requires consideration of the marketplace, staff capabilities, and compatibility with hospital goals. Also, prepackaged modules may be the answer for hospitals with low program funding. There are a number of such programs available and likely will be more in the future. One unique arrangement is provided by the National Center for Health Promotion, a for-profit company which trains hospital staff using its own materials and protocol in specific content areas (smoking, weight control, and stress management), then franchises the hospital as sole marketer of the programs in a particular geographic area.

5. Evaluation. What can be offered to the corporate purchaser in the way of concrete program results? Obviously, most companies investing in health promotion are looking for tangible results. They will seek such results from whomever they choose to purchase the services. Also, evidence supporting the efficacy of the program is a powerful marketing tool.

6. Sales and Marketing. Most hospitals are not capable of sophisticated marketing and sales techniques. To successfully initiate a program, new staff will likely need to be hired. Too often hospitals try to create and staff new programs by reassigning personnel from other departments. This method will work only if the transferred employee has both the expertise and a strong interest in health promotion.

In the rush to establish health promotion programs targeted toward the corporate community, hospitals have neglected their most natural clientele—hospital patients. The typical patient is at a uniquely teachable moment. And since most patients are in the hospital for a lifestyle-related reason, health promoting efforts can be especially appropriate. The cardiac patient, just having undergone bypass surgery, is ready and motivated as never before to avoid future medical problems.

Many opportunities exist to direct patients towards health and wellness classes after discharge. Consider the following hypothetical program.

As part of their standard admissions procedures most hospitals collect all the information necessary to complete a standardized health risk appraisal (HRA). With this information, the clerk completes an HRA and obtains results for each patient. With the recent conversion of HRA programs to the microcomputer, the hospital no longer needs to purchase the inventories from outside vendors. Also, results can be obtained immediately. The results, in addition to providing an individual with information about his or her major risks and how those risks can be reduced, also include a referral list of hospital-sponsored, health enhancing programs. The patient's physician can enter the process by helping with the interpretation of the HRA results and encouraging patient participation in an ongoing program. The costs for this program would be quite low (perhaps less than $10), but the potential for substantial financial benefit to the hospital and improved health for the patient is high.

Another little used patient education tool is television. Since most patient rooms are equipped with televisions, numerous opportunities exist for reaching the patients with health information and news of hospital programs. Someday soon, the patient will be able to interact with the television by filling out questionnaires right from the bed. Also, tapes of programs could be rented from the hospital for use in the rooms or at home just as you would a feature film.

A hospital health promotion can fit well with other corporate health programs consistent with the goals of most hospitals. Examples of related programs are employee assistance programs and occupational health programs, such as hearing conservation, back education, and return to work programs for disability cases. All of these and others can be packaged together providing a comprehensive corporate program of health maintenance enhancement.

EAPs are a particularly good entry point for hospitals because the benefits to the corporation can be shown in dollars and cents within a relatively short time. Evaluating the use of the EAP will also indicate areas of employee problems, whether they are drugs, alcohol, stress, etc. These will, in turn, suggest which health promoting programs should be designed to meet specific needs.

Community Health Promotion Programs

The majority of established health promotion programs are directed at employees at the work site and students in colleges and universities. There are significant numbers of people in most communities not served by such programs. Senior citizens, school children, the unemployed, the poor, and employees of very small organizations represent a major portion of any community population. Community-based health promotion programs are an ideal vehicle to provide health enhancing services to this population group.

The concept of community health promotion is still very new. Few formal programs exist to serve all of the sectors of the community. However, the concept is a valuable one which is likely to grow rapidly in the future. There will be impetus to coordinate programs as more community organizations and agencies seek to initiate health promoting services to their specific constituencies. Hospitals are the traditional health care providers in the community and can have a major role in this new development.

Most communities have numerous organizations which, to some degree, are dedicated to the improvement of the health of their members. Examples which are common to most communities include the YMCA/YWCA, elementary and secondary schools, day care centers, city recreation departments, senior citizens housing and activity programs, city and county health departments, and local hospitals and clinics.

A community hospital can take the lead for a community program by soliciting interest from among the leaders of organizations and political entities in the community. Because of the relative newness of the concept of community wellness, there are no proven strategies to guide the formation of such programs. Clearly, however, the pooling of resources available in most cities and towns has the potential for significant health-enhancing impact. Three communities which have made efforts to coordinate health promotion programs for all community members are Sheboygan, Wisconsin, Athens, GA, and Stevens Point, Wisconsin.

— 11 —

Wellness in Colleges and Universities

Colleges have long been concerned about issues affecting students beyond the classroom. It was clear to early American college faculty that there had to be concern for more than the intellectual growth of students. Self-discovery, psychological well being, values and morals, religious interest, refinement of tastes, practical competence for citizenship and economic productivity were all concerns of university faculties. At the turn of this century, it became common practice for colleges to have on their staff a full-time administrator, called the Dean of Students, who was concerned with these issues. It was the role of this person to define the extracurricular parameters for the student body and monitor and enforce university rules. As the years went by, the functions associated with this office grew and became specialized into such diverse functional areas as counseling, career planning and placement, health services, residence life, university student unions, and the like. The overriding philosophical basis for the varied activities of the Student Affairs staff became known as in loco parentis. This philosophy, which explicitly defined appropriate student behavior outside the classroom, was an important feature of Student Affairs well into the 1950s. As Student Affairs Divisions became more expansive and diverse, and they also became more separated from what is traditionally considered the primary function of the college—teaching.

In the past 20 years, a new concept of the role of the Student Affairs staff in colleges and universities has emerged. This philosophy, known as student development, sees students as whole persons and recognizes the need for universities and colleges to be concerned not only with the intellectual growth and development of students but also with their emotional and psychomotor development. Important features of this model include:

1. The notion that human development is a continuous and cumulative process of physical, psychological and social growth which may be divided into stages
2. Development occurs when change is anticipated and planned for
3. Systematic integration of cognitive, affective, and psychomotor experiences produces most effective development
4. Development is enhanced when students, faculty, and staff work collaboratively to promote continuous development.

More recently, writers have put forth the notion of "intentionality," the idea of "developing a plan for promoting the kinds of developmental learning and skills that students have identified as desirable for their own life purposes" (Miller and Prince, 1977). Emphasis is placed on the involvement of students in determining their needs and directing their own development with the assistance of professionals. Miller and Prince go on to say that "the intent is to meet individuals where they are developmentally and help them move on from there." In their model of student development, they identify six basic components:

- Goal setting
- Assessment

- Instruction
- Consultation
- Milieu management
- Evaluation

The target populations for their model are individuals, groups, and organizations. Of course, few campuses have actually achieved these lofty ideals. Traditional student affairs departments such as counseling centers, health services, and student conduct offices are most often dealing with student problems. Table 11.1 contrasts these different models of student development.

It should become obvious to the reader that many of the ideas described as student development parallel closely the culturing philosophy of life-style change put forth in this book. Therefore, colleges and universities, or at least those who have taken seriously the precepts of student development theory, are in an ideal position to move directly into a wellness process. Wellness is based on the multi-dimensionality and interdependence of six dimensions including the occupational, emotional, spiritual, social, intellectual and physical dimensions. It does not require a great philosophical shift to move from a perspective which views students as integrated wholes incorporating the intellectual, emotional, and psychomotor dimensions to one which incorporates a multi-dimensional wellness process.

A University Model—The University of Wisconsin-Stevens Point

The first formally established wellness program on a university campus was developed at the University of Wisconsin-Stevens Point in 1972. The approach used to implement this wellness program over the past decade has become the model adopted by dozens of other colleges and universities throughout the United States. The program at Stevens Point originally grew from, and is primarily directed by, the University's Student Life Division. Wellness has been defined as the overall mission of the Student Life area. The mission statement reads, "This mission is seen as consistent with and supportive of the overall goals of the university and is accomplished in the Student Life area through human development programming" (UWSP, 1983). As this statement suggests, the wellness model has been melded with the more traditional student development models adopted by many other universities.

An important characteristic of the Stevens Point model is that it has become a functional part of virtually all of the many student affairs departments. In addition to the obvious areas, such as the Health Service and the Counseling Center, programs with a wellness emphasis are found in Residence Life, Student Life Activities and Programs, University Centers, and Business Operations. Wellness curricula have recently been adopted in the

Table 11.1   Contrasting Campus Models*

	Traditional	Health Promotion	Wellness
Primary Goal	Identify and Correct Problem	Disease Prevention and Risk Reduction	Health Creation
Dominant Message	We will take care of you	It's fun avoiding illness. If you do, you will live longer	You are responsible, and the university supports your efforts to be well
Change Agent	Treatment	Information and behavior change	Positive experience and cultural influences
Target	The Problem	Students by Risk Factors	Students Within Cultures
Duration of Intervention	Until Problems clears up	Length of class or program	Ongoing part of culture

*Adapted from a model by Hipp and Opatz, 1983.

academic departments of Physical Education, Health Education, Nutrition, and Psychology.

Fred Leafgren, Assistant Chancellor for Student Life, and the person responsible for establishing the wellness mission at Stevens Point, suggests 11 strategies for coordinating all Student Life services to enhance wellness opportunities.

Strategy One. Establish administrative leadership and support. The task of initiating a university-wide program is made substantially easier when the administrator responsible for all non-academic student programs is solidly behind the wellness approach. Through careful selection and training of key staff, the implementation and coordination of wellness programs are made possible. Support for the programs should be communicated to staff both verbally and in writing. Credibility is further established by key leadership taking an active personal interest in the process.

Strategy Two. Inventory existing programs to identify those programs presently serving the wellness function. Undoubtedly, every institution has many current programs successfully meeting the goals of a potential wellness program. One of the first and most important steps in creating the university program is to identify these programs. Once identified, they can be recognized as part of the newly established wellness effort. At the same time, any overlap or duplication of effort, can be minimized. Examples of current programs serving a wellness function might include health education courses through the health center, leadership training programs through student activities, and recreational activities sponsored by intramural programs.

Strategy Three. Identify staff who are interested in and are living a wellness lifestyle. One of the immediate needs of the new program will be to establish a planning and implementation process. A committee designed for such a purpose will ideally be composed of members who have a professional and personal interest in one or more of the components of the wellness philosophy. Other staff can be drawn into program implementation by providing activities and services which are consistent with their areas of expertise.

Strategy Four. Identify students already interested and committed to a wellness lifestyle. To be consistent with a philosophy which encourages participation on the part of those for whom programs are directed, members of the student body should participate in the planning process. With some training, many students can become instructors in peer programs. In this way, many more students can be reached and valuable staff time conserved.

Strategy Five. Bring all existing personnel resources together for a meeting early in the planning process. It will be useful to reach consensus on program priorities and directions. A meeting, or meetings, at which brainstorming and goal setting can occur will be most valuable. Faculty and other non-student affairs administrators should also be encouraged to participate. For most institutions, the early stages of the program will be modest in their scope. Support by the broadest cross section of the institution will assure that these early efforts are successful.

Strategy Six. Involve all student affairs units in a partnership for wellness program implementation. It is not necessary to create new organizational structures in order to implement the program. Rather, existing student affairs units can be called upon to integrate the overall wellness mission into their particular functional area. There are, obviously, some units which have more in common with the wellness program than do others. These should be encouraged to give special attention to its implementation. However, this does not mean that areas such as new student orientation, career services, admissions, and food services cannot play a valuable role in the development of program strategies.

Strategy Seven. Identify other campus resources available to assist in the comprehensive wellness program development. One of the six dimensions of the wellness philosophy at Stevens Point is the intellectual dimension. Identification and inclusion of academic courses and activities in the wellness effort enables the program to achieve its holistic goals. One way to accomplish this is by asking each academic department to inventory its programs and services and identify those which may be related to the wellness philosophy, if only tangentially. In this way, the task of implementing a comprehensive program can be more easily realized.

Strategy Eight. Inform students and faculty about the program and their opportunities. Communicating program goals and activities to students is best accomplished when information comes from numerous sources, in many formats and all the time. At Stevens Point, the student is constantly made aware of the wellness lifestyle through regular publications, assessment tools, and programs. Food and nutrition options through the food service, contact with the health service, posters, films, contests, and many other effective marketing methods are used regularly.

Strategy Nine. Establish a priority for implementing the various facets of the total comprehensive program. It will be necessary to determine which goals can be met immediately and which must be deferred over a longer period of time. No institution can expect to plan, implement, and gain acceptance for a full blown health promotion program within a year or even in two. Careful selection of goals and the activities for their accomplishment will assure a gradual achievement of program objectives. The Stevens Point program started out on a much more modest scale than is now apparent. Commitment and ownership of the current program has taken years of development.

Strategy Ten. Provide adequate training for professional staff and students involved in implementing the program. The development and maintenance of wellness skills requires both an orientation to the wellness philosophy and periodic-skill building sessions. In the early stages of program development, it may be useful to bring in an outside consultant or send staff members to appropriate conferences. At Stevens Point, particular attention is paid to the training of residence hall and health service staff. Students are also involved in the process. Many are aspiring to careers in health promotion or related fields. Proper training enables the programs initiated to reach a far wider audience.

Strategy Eleven. Evaluate the programs that are being implemented for comprehensive wellness. Only through systematic assessments can the worth of programs be determined. Given the limited resources available for health promotion in most institutions, the evaluation process becomes critical in determining where those resources are to be expended. When possible, formal research on health promotion programs in the university setting should be undertaken to determine their effectiveness in helping students to reach developmental goals.

Introducing Students to Wellness

Students, as freshmen entering the University of Wisconsin-Stevens Point, become familiar with the wellness concept before their first day of college. As is typical in most colleges, incoming students are required to submit to a traditional physical examination. This examination, often perfunctory, and with little real benefit to the average 18-year-old, was partially abandoned in favor of a more educational screening program involving a health risk appraisal. At Stevens Point, all students are given the option to either submit to a traditional physical examination (at considerable cost and inconvenience) or complete a questionnaire (a small fee is charged). The first questionnaire used was one purchased from a for-profit enterprise. In addition to being expensive, the information it provided was primarily risk related rather than emphasizing lifestyle choice. The purchased questionnaire was eventually replaced by a more comprehensive instrument developed, after considerable work and expense, by university staff called the Lifestyle Assessment Questionnaire (LAQ).

The LAQ, now in its third edition, is chosen over the physical exam by more than 90 percent of the incoming freshmen. This unusual approach provides the foundation for all other wellness interventions during the student's next four years. Prior to stepping foot on campus, the student is introduced to the concept of wellness and its significance in the community the student is about to enter. In addition, the LAQ is designed so that it becomes the first document in the student's health service file and the basis for wellness programs during the first weeks of school.

As part of the matriculation process, students receive the LAQ results during "group interpretation sessions" conducted in the residence halls by trained residence hall staff. The sessions provide an opportunity to discuss and fully understand individual results and to set objectives for making desired health-related behavior changes. The session also serves as an important opportunity for freshmen to meet and interact socially with their peers during their first days of college.

Student Health Center

Many of the wellness-related activities at Stevens Point emanate from the Student Health Center. Students entering the Center for the first time find an environment quite different from that of their hometown clinics. In addition to a very informal atmosphere, void of white coats and the smell of disinfectant, the student is confronted with an environment rich in health education materials and learning opportunities. Instead of soap operas, the waiting room television shows high-quality videotapes on subjects ranging from birth control methods to personal relationships. Micro-computer programs, blood pressure screening devices, and numerous other wellness related materials are available to the waiting student.

Students are frequently asked to get involved in their own illness care. For example, students complaining of cold symptoms are not seen by a physician or other health care professional but, rather, are directed to the Cold Clinic. The Cold Clinic is a self assessment program containing a series of stations located in the waiting room. After reading instructions, examining their throats, and taking their temperatures, students complete a prescription form and submit it to the pharmacist at the last station. In addition to teaching students an important lesson in self care, the Cold Clinic relieves the Health Service staff from dealing with the most frequent medical complaint of college age adults.

The Health Center's role goes far beyond responding to the needs of the ill or injured student. The Wellness Model extends from the Health Service to all campus areas. The Health Service is the only department at the University to have a professional on staff who is dedicated specifically to health promotion. This wellness coordinator is responsible for the publication of a Wellness Newsletter, the food service nutrition programs, and the development of materials disseminating health information. But most important to the coordinator's job is the training and supervision of a team of students called Lifestyle Assistants.

The Lifestyle Assistant Program was initiated in 1980 so that greater numbers of students would have opportunities to engage in health promoting programs and activities. Since the number of health service staff members is limited and their first commitment is to students seeking illness care, they can have only limited contact and impact on the well-being of the largely healthy student community. Therefore, a contingent of students (usually between 10 and 15) is hired each year to initiate programs for fellow students. After a period of intensive training by the wellness coordinator and other Health Service staff, the Lifestyle Assistants (known as LAs) develop, promote, and lead wellness programs of their own choice in the residence halls and the Health Services and University Centers. The most popular programs include aerobic dancing, weight reduction, stress management, and fitness assessments.

The response to LA-sponsored programs has been overwhelmingly positive. In 1982, over 200 programs attended by 2,000 students were developed and completed by the LAs. This level of activity would be impossible using only paid professional staff. (See Appendix D for a listing of Health Service and other Student Life sponsored programs.)

Creating a Healthy Campus Culture

In addition to making many behavior change programs available to the students, a concentrated effort has been initiated to effect positive changes in the campus environment. Educating students about the effects of alcohol, nutrition, and cigarette smoking are three examples of such efforts. Alcohol consumption is an important part of the central Wisconsin culture. Though alcohol consumption is allowed on campus, its consumption is closely regulated. Every effort is made to promote its use only in social situations. Alternative beverages are always available and moderate consumption is acceptable. An example of an explicit alcohol policy can be seen at the bottom of the menu for Jeremiah's, a drinking and eating establishment in the University Center. It states, "Jeremiah's was designed as a peaceful environment, an alternative establishment where social interaction, fun and fellowship prevail. For this reason, we choose not to serve intoxicated people. We ask for everyone's cooperation in this effort."

Alcohol abuse is certainly not absent from campus. However, when it does occur, it is dealt with directly. "Passing out" from over-consumption of alcohol is considered a medical emergency and paramedics are called to take the student to the hospital emergency room.

Policies regarding cigarette smoking on campus anticipated a movement by enlightened state legislators in various parts of the country by adopting policies which protect the rights of non-smokers. Smoking is allowed only in designated smoking areas and many of the Student Life offices have no place for smoking whatsoever.

Special attention is given to the food available to students. Since almost half of the student population lives in residence halls and, therefore, eats three meals a day provided by the University, the food program can have a powerful impact on healthy nutrition choices. The Food Service contract is negotiated to include provision for high quality fresh fruits, vegetables, and whole grain foods. In addition, all entrees are labeled as to their fat, carbohydrate, and protein content. Special effort is made to train the cooks and food preparers in the basic principles of nutrition and new methods of cooking. These efforts certainly do not preclude the opportunity for students to select less than ideal food. However, the philosophy is that students should at least have the opportunity to make healthy food choices.

Wellness as an Academic Endeavor

As is the case in most universities, UWSP includes courses in health education and physical education as part of its general education requirements. In the past, a required course in health education typically meant learning about personal hygiene and health maintenance concepts through text books. Students could also make selections from among numerous physical education classes which typically included such skill sports as badminton, basketball, volleyball, and tennis. A traditional health education course has been replaced by a wellness course which emphasizes the importance of self responsibility and lifestyle choices. In addition to textbook learning, students have an opportunity to experience, through lifestyle assessments, fitness testing and other mechanisms, new life skills which will be with them long after the course has ended. In the fitness courses, opportunities are provided which emphasize cardiovascular health in sports or activities and which can be maintained over a lifetime. Sports such as running, cross-country skiing, bicycling, aerobic dance, and swimming are now important parts of the physical education curriculum.

Wellness courses are not limited to the Physical Education Department. The Psychology Department also offers courses focusing on psychological well-being, stress management, and personal relationships.

The University of Wisconsin-Stevens Point is one of the first universities in the country to initiate an academic major in health promotion. The growing demand for trained professionals in this field has created a need for formal programs training students for entry into this career field. The interdisciplinary program, including courses in psychology, physical education, health education, and business, is receiving strong interest from students.

Though the University of Wisconsin-Stevens Point has had a wellness program longer than any other university, there are numerous other campuses involved in wellness in many different ways.

— 12 —

Conclusion: The Future of Health Promotion

The progress made by the health promotion movement is remarkable. Within a span of less than 10 years we have witnessed changes propelling the field from the idea stage to a practical, society-wide phenomenon. Several factors have fueled the health promotion movement—the running boom and increased interest in personal health, high health care costs coupled with a reduced return on that investment, the change in the work force from one primarily dedicated to manufacturing to a preponderance of service industries. The health promotion movement appears to be here to stay.

Signs of continued growth are apparent. More and larger conferences on all aspects of health and wellness are being conducted. The National Wellness Conference, once the only such conference in the country, has seen an increase in participation each year since its inception nine years ago. Other similar conferences are being conducted on a regional basis to serve the increased demand for information, ideas, and contact with colleagues. In Minnesota, a hotbed of health promotion, an informal network of health promotion professionals has been created for the sole purpose of sharing information in this rapidly changing field.

The Organization of Wellness Networks (OWN), an outgrowth of the National Wellness Conference in 1981, has steadily increased in membership. In 1984, it published the first professional journal, Wellness Perspectives, dedicated exclusively to health promotion. Other organizations with goals originally tangential to health promotion have been expanding their areas of interest and concern to include health promotion issues. Particularly noteworthy in this regard are the American Alliance of Health, Physical Education, Recreation, and Dance (AAHPERD), and the rapidly growing Association for Fitness in Business (AFB).

The next 10 to 20 years are likely to see growth of the health promotion field as rapid as that in the recent past. The programs now being initiated with adult populations, particularly in the work setting, are remedial in nature. That is, most programs are designed as corrective actions for destructive behaviors already learned. There is growing interest in health promotion programs for the younger population—in schools, communities, and universities. This suggests that rather than remedial, programs with adult populations in the future will focus on maintenance and support for already acquired healthy lifestyles. Parents will continue to have a powerful impact on the future health of their children. Adult programs can be especially effective by providing training and parenting skills designed to promote positive lifestyle behaviors before a child reaches school age.

Concerns for the Future

Though the future of health promotion appears assured, there will no doubt be critical hurdles to overcome. There will be increasing tension created as new health care delivery systems and the monies to support them diminish the resources currently expended in traditional health care areas. Already we are witnessing the early signs of this tension. Many hospitals are beginning to experience reduced occupancies due to shorter patient stays, HMO growth, and other cost containment strategies. In addition, recent health statistics show a decline in heart disease and cancer, two important revenue generating maladies. To make matters worse for hospitals, in 1984 Congress initiated a program to hold down costs by establishing a flat rate reimbursement system for Medicare. The impact has been a drastic reduction in hospital revenues.

A precedent setting strike by 6,000 nurses against 18 hospitals in the Minneapolis-St. Paul area during the spring of 1984 was directly attributable to the financial squeeze caused by cost containment efforts. The response by the hospitals to the problem was to lay off large numbers of nurses and negotiate for greater flexibility and reduced seniority rights to make future layoffs easier. Other metropolitan areas can expect similar problems soon.

As the health promotion field continues to grow, its credibility and legitimacy as an important social movement will be put to the test. Health promotion advocates, who promote the possibility of improved societal health in terms of increased life expectancy and enhanced individual well-being, must be cautious to make claims of its efficacy no greater than the current scientific evidence will allow. Already, health promotion has been accepted by many individuals in institutions who initially suspected it of being no more than a fad, born in California, and doomed to obscurity on short notice.

However, in the excitement over tentative findings and preliminary results based primarily on correlational studies, many in the field are over-selling health promotion as a panacea. In a thoughtful analysis of the current data supporting health promotion programming, Kaplan (1984) finds reason for optimism but recommends caution in overstating the benefits of health promotion. He concludes by saying:

> "Many current activities in health promotion are supported by the best available empirical evidence. Programs to prevent common problems such as heart disease should be continued. My only concern is that we recognize the complexities of the problems and the general absence of definitive evidence on the relationship between behavioral intervention and disease prevention. There is no quarrel with health promotion, only with the promotion of health promotion."

The greatest threat to the credibility and wide acceptance of the health promotion movement comes not from the overzealous practitioners convinced of the importance of risk reduction programs as a means to improved health. Rather, the threat comes from charlatans, quacks, con artists and the ill-informed representing products and services which at best represent the scientific fringes and strain the credulity of even the most open minded. Unfortunately, medicine and related health fields have always been plagued with more than their share of false promises. Miracle cures, potions, and elixers are as prevalent today as ever before. One need only look in any popular magazine to find ads for such products as instant weight loss pills, chelation therapy, iridology, aura readings, and untested megavitamin regimens.

Unproven products and services are by no means limited to the physical dimension of health. The study of the so-called mind-body connection, now only in its infancy, offers tremendous potential as a powerful health maintenance and restorative tool. But the claims for the benefits to be obtained from many of the methods put forth to psychologically manipulate the body back to health are yet to be proven. Applied kinesiology, rolfing, EST and other modalities which reference some as yet unsubstantiated "psychic energy field" as the be-all and end-all to total health threaten the important findings and potential of the emerging health promotion field.

Unfortunately many in the field, anxious for new program ideas, are too easily impressed by the slick presentations of spokespersons attempting to sell their unique and "important" new methods. And, of course, as consumers, we all wish to obtain optimal health with the least amount of pain and suffering. How much easier to have needles stuck in one's ear than to go through an agonizing and extended withdrawal from cigarettes!

The evidence supporting preventative health-promoting lifestyles is already sizeable and will continue to grow. There is no need to make exaggerated claims for the benefits of wellness. A skeptical, cautious, but open-minded approach will continue to be the best position from which to assess new and promising health-enhancing methods.

The Changing Work Site

American industry is experiencing a change no less profound than that resulting from the Industrial Revolution. Alvin Toffler refers to this dramatic shift in society as the Third Wave, his recent book. We have already experienced some of these changes. An ever smaller number of workers are engaged in manual labor directed at the production of products and goods. Increasingly, the work force is composed of white collar office workers involved in information creation and exchange. This shift from the production of products to production of information and services has profound implications for the relationship of workers to their employers with respect to worker health. Safety is no longer the paramount concern that it has been during the past 50 years. New issues revolving around satisfaction with the work, job enrichment, opportunities to experience and practice different lifestyles, and personal autonomy are becoming important. Employees are demanding an active role in the development of programs designed to improve their health and quality of life, and organizations are responding positively.

Employees are seen as having a collective impact on the success of the organization that they never had before. This collective impact is seen as the result of shared values which drive the company towards successful goal attainment or failure. Companies have responded by systematically attempting to define and focus the values and culture of their organizations with respect to their goals. An inconsistency between employee values and organizational objectives is perceived to be debilitating. This new approach, in contrast to the scientific management and human resource movements of the early century, is creating organizations which are more responsive to the needs and interests of their members without compromising long-term goals. This change in strategy has affected the day-to-day operations of many organizations. A good example is that of Intel Corporation. Its President, Andrew Grove, contrasts his style of management with historical precedent (1984). Because of rapidly changing technologies, those individuals in positions of power (executives and upper level management) are no longer the same individuals with the knowledge necessary to produce new products. Thus, in order to stay competitive, frequent and informal interaction between the "knowledge-power people" and the "position-power people" is required. The knowledge-power people are generally younger, highly trained technicians with recently acquired skills in the relevant knowledge area. These junior members must participate with senior managers in the decision-making process in order for the organization to succeed. Traditional symbols of corporate power must be shed in order to promote this sharing of power. In the case of Intel, this has meant small functional offices for everyone including the chief executive, no special perquisites in terms of cars and parking spaces and an emphasis on access to all organizational members on a regular basis.

This change in the relationship among the levels of the corporate hierarchy represents nothing less than a revolution in organizational development. Promoting health and lifestyle change as a corporate strategy for organizational enhancement, represents a similar "paradigm shift," a term coined by Thomas Coon in the Structure of Science Revolutions (1970). In its original context, a paradigm shift was an occasion when accepted axioms of science were replaced overnight with a revolutionary new approach or understanding. Marilyn Ferguson (1980) argues that we are in the midst of a political paradigm shift which questions past governmental and social customs. Organizations are also experiencing a powerful movement toward acceptance and encouragement of individual choices which will ultimately improve and sustain both individual and organizational health.

Instead of building skyscrapers and edifices to corporate founders, we are constructing office buildings which provide an environment that supports the growing numbers of white collar workers and is dominated by the quiet whirr of computer terminals rather than the clank and rattle of dangerous industrial machinery. A whole new set of issues, from the technical to the psychological, is being raised. By 1990 it is estimated that over half of all office workers will be using computer terminals and that by the year 2000, 90 percent of all workers will hold white collar jobs. The new science of ergonomics, the design of work stations physically and psychologically appropriate to the individual, has arrived. Employees will work with less strain and greater comfort. Concurrently, efforts are being made to create informal, less structured, and more personal work environments with softer lighting, quieter work space, and visually appealing surroundings. Clearly, health promotion professionals are faced with challenges and opportunities far beyond the provision of risk reduction programs.

APPENDICES

APPENDIX A

Sample Health Risk Inventory

*COMPUTE—A—LIFE II©

This questionnaire is designed to help you discover risks that are likely to interfere with your living a long and healthy life. Once you know your risks you may choose to avoid many of them by making changes in the way you live. By making the recommended changes you increase your chances of living longer and better.

The data stored in this program have been collected from literally millions of American death certificates. Over the past twenty years millions of people have died prematurely. Carefully supervised research projects have shown that the vast majority of these deaths were the direct result of lifestyle choices.

Record your answers on the accompanying answer card. Your responses will be scored by a computer, so please darken the spaces carefully. If you change an answer, erase completely. The computer can only read a No. 2 pencil.

Developed for students of the University of Wisconsin-Stevens Point through a grant from **Metropolitan Life Foundation.**
*Compute-A-Life II is a product of the Institute for Lifestyle Improvement and is reprinted here with permission.

Answer the following questions carefully.

1. Are you
   A. Male
   B. Female

2. Which race are you a member of?
   A. White
   B. Black
   C. Other

3. Which category best describes your physical activity?
   A. I am sedentary at work and leisure
   B. I get a little exercise at work or at home
   C. I exercise once or twice a week
   D. I exercise 3 times a week for at least 20 minutes each time
   E. I exercise vigorously more than 3 times a week

4. Your blood pressure is an important indicator of your health. Blood pressure is measured with two numbers; the systolic number is first, followed by the diastolic number. For example, a good blood pressure is 110/70. What is your systolic number? If it is below 120, please leave blank.
   A. 200
   B. 180
   C. 160
   D. 140
   E. 120

5. What is your diastolic number? If your diastolic blood pressure is below 85, please leave blank.
   A. 105
   B. 100
   C. 95
   D. 90
   E. 85

6. Which category describes your present weight?
   A. Underweight
   B. Average ... + or − 5%
   C. 6%–20% overweight
   D. 21%–50% overweight
   E. More than 50% overweight

7. In terms of alcohol consumption, how would you describe yourself? Leave blank if you consume no alcohol.

		Drinks per week:
A.	Alcoholic	40+
B.	Heavy drinker	25–39
C.	Mild excess	7–24
D.	Moderate	2–7

E. Used to drink, but stopped, or infrequent social drinker.

8. A high cholesterol level is associated with increased risk for cardiovascular disease. What is your cholesterol level? If you don't know, leave blank. An average number for age, race and sex will be used.
   A. Above 250
   B. 221–250
   C. 201–220
   D. 180–200
   E. Less than 180

9. How many miles do you drive/ride a year?
   (The average driver/rider travels 10,000 miles a year.)
   A. 3,000–5,000
   B. 5,000–10,000
   C. 10,000–20,000
   D. 20,000–30,000
   E. over 30,000

10. Of the time spent in a vehicle, what percent do you wear a seat belt?
    A. 0% of the time
    B. 1%–33%
    C. 34%–66%
    D. 67%–99%
    E. 100% of the time

11. Which category best describes the drinking habits of people you normally drive with?

		Drinks per week
A.	Heavy drinker	25+
B.	Mild excess	7–24
C.	Moderate	1–6
D.	Non drinker	

E. Never ride with a drinking driver

12. For whatever reasons, do you carry a weapon?
    A. Yes
    B. No

13. Which statement describes your arrest record?
    A. I've been arrested for burglary, robbery, or assault.
    B. I've been arrested for non-violent crime other than traffic-related offenses.
    C. I've been arrested for traffic violation(s) with a fine greater than $75.
    D. I've never been arrested, other than for minor traffic violations.

14. Which category describes your usual state of depression?
    A. Frequently depressed
    B. Often depressed
    C. Sometimes depressed
    D. Seldom depressed
    E. Never depressed

15. Do you now use tobacco in any form?
    A. Yes—skip to question 18
    B. No

16. Have you ever used tobacco in any form?
    A. Yes
    B. No—skip to question 19

17. If you no longer use tobacco, congratulations. How long ago did you quit?
    A. Less than one year ago
    B. 1–4 years ago
    C. 5 years ago or more

18. In what amount do/did you use tobacco?
    A. Very heavy (40 cigarettes a day or equivalent)
    B. Heavy (20–39)
    C. Moderate (10–19)
    D. Light (1–9)

19. Do you have emphysema?
    A. Yes
    B. No

20. Have you had rheumatic fever?
    A. Yes, and I am not on medication
    B. Yes, and I take medication as a result
    C. No

21. Have you ever had undiagnosed rectal bleeding?
    A. Yes
    B. No

22. Are you diabetic?
    A. Yes, and it's uncontrolled
    B. Yes, and it's controlled
    C. No

23. Polyps are little finger-like projections found inside places like your intestines. Have you had polyps?
    A. Yes
    B. No

24. Bacterial pneumonia, in contrast to the more common viral pneumonia, is likely to recur. Have you ever had bacterial pneumonia?
    A. Yes
    B. No

25. Which statement describes the lifespan of your parents?
    A. Neither parent lived beyond 70 years of age
    B. One parent alive and lived beyond 70 years of age
    C. Both parents still living and under 70 years of age
    D. Both parents alive and lived beyond 70 years of age

26. Do you have a family history of diabetes? (Consider your parents, brothers, and sisters)
    A. Yes
    B. No

27. Have there been any suicides or attempted suicides in your immediate family?
    A. Yes
    B. No

28. Have you had ulcerative colitis?
    A. No
    B. Yes, for less than 10 years
    C. Yes, for 10 years or more

The remaining questions pertain only to women.
Men, return your questionnaire and answer card. You will have your results soon.

29. Have you ever had fibrocystic disease?
    A. Yes
    B. No

30. Which statement applies to your family history of breast cancer? Consider only your mother and sisters.
    A. Two or more family members have had breast cancer
    B. One family member has had breast cancer
    C. No family member has had breast cancer

31. Do you have an annual breast exam by a health professional?
    A. Yes
    B. No

32. Select the category that describes your menstrual status
    A. Still menstruating
    B. Natural menopause before 45
    C. Natural menopause 45 and over
    D. Surgical menopause before 35
    E. Surgical menopause 35 and over

33. Have you had unexplained vaginal bleeding between your periods?
    A. Yes
    B. No

34. Which statement best describes your pap smear results?
    A. I've had one negative pap smear in the last 5 years
    B. I've had one negative pap smear in the last year
    C. I've had 3 negative pap smears in the last 5 years
    D. My annual tests have been negative and I plan to continue having a pap smear every year
    E. I've never had a pap smear

35. Cervical cancer is related to early sexual intercourse. Which statement best describes your onset of sexual activity?
    A. As a teenager
    B. 20–25
    C. Over 25
    D. Never

36. Economic status is also related to cervical cancer. Which of the following best describes your economic status?
    A. Low
    B. Average
    C. High

Sample Results

Marlene Q. Dieterich

Actual age = = >   38

Current health age = = >   38
Achievable health age = = >   33

—TOP TEN CAUSES OF DEATH FOR YOUR AGE, RACE, AND SEX—
1) Breast Cancer
2) Arteriosclerotic Heart Disease
3) Suicide
4) Motor Vehicle Accidents
5) Vascular Lesions of the Central Nervous System (Stroke)
6) Cirrhosis
7) Lung Cancer
8) Homicide
9) Cancer of the Large Intestine and Rectum
10) Cancer of the Cervix

APPENDIX B

Sample Wellness Inventory

TestWell
A Self-Scoring
Wellness Assessment Questionnaire

TestWell was developed by Joseph P. Opatz and William Hettler and is copyrighted by the Institute for Lifestyle Improvement (1984).

Physical Fitness

1. I exercise aerobically (continuous, vigorous exercise producing sweat for a minimum of thirty minutes) at least ___per week.
   1 = five times 2 = four times 3 = three times
   4 = two times 5 = less than twice

   ANSWER = [1 2 3 4 5]

2. My resting pulse rate is ___beats per minute.
   1 = 40 to 55   2 = 56 to 69 3 = 70 to 79
   4 = 80 or above   5 = don't know

   ANSWER = [1 2 3 4 5]

3. I avoid the extremes of too much or too little exercise
   1 = strongly agree 2 = agree 3 = neutral/not sure
   4 = disagree   5 = strongly disagree

   ANSWER = [1 2 3 4 5]

4. I approach exercise in a relaxed manner
   1 = almost always 2 = very frequently 3 = frequently
   4 = occasionally   5 = almost never

   ANSWER = [1 2 3 4 5]

5. I stretch before exercising.
   1 = almost always 2 = very frequently 3 = frequently
   4 = occasionally   5 = almost never

   ANSWER = [1 2 3 4 5]

6. I stretch after exercising.
   1 = almost always 2 = very frequently 3 = frequently
   4 = occasionally   5 = almost never

   ANSWER = [1 2 3 4 5]

7. I increase my exercise by walking or biking whenever possible.
   1 = strongly agree 2 = agree 3 = neutral/not sure
   4 = disagree   5 = strongly disagree

   ANSWER = [1 2 3 4 5]

8. I get an adequate amount of sleep.
   1 = almost always 2 = very frequently 3 = frequently
   4 = occasionally   5 = almost never

   ANSWER = [1 2 3 4 5]

9. My exercise program includes an adequate amount of each of the three major fitness components—endurance, strength, and flexibility.
    1 = almost always   2 = very frequently   3 = frequently
    4 = occasionally   5 = almost never

    ANSWER = | 1 | 2 | 3 | 4 | 5 |

10. If I am not in shape, I avoid sporadic (once a week or less) strenuous exercise.
    1 = almost always   2 = very frequently   3 = frequently
    4 = occasionally   5 = almost never

    ANSWER = | 1 | 2 | 3 | 4 | 5 |

    TOTAL = | 1 | 2 | 3 | 4 | 5 |

Nutrition

Check.   1 = almost always   2 = very frequently   3 = frequently
          4 = occasionally   5 = almost never

ANSWER = | 1 | 2 | 3 | 4 | 5 |

1. When choosing non-vegetable protein, I select lean cuts of meat, poultry, and fish.

    ANSWER = | 1 | 2 | 3 | 4 | 5 |

2. I minimize salt intake.

    ANSWER = | 1 | 2 | 3 | 4 | 5 |

3. I eat fruit and vegetables fresh and uncooked.

    ANSWER = | 1 | 2 | 3 | 4 | 5 |

4. I eat breakfast.

    ANSWER = | 1 | 2 | 3 | 4 | 5 |

5. I intentionally include fiber in my diet on a daily basis.

    ANSWER = | 1 | 2 | 3 | 4 | 5 |

6. I drink enough fluid to keep my urine light yellow.

    ANSWER = | 1 | 2 | 3 | 4 | 5 |

7. I plan my diet to insure an adequate amount of vitamins and minerals.

1 2 3 4 5
ANSWER = ⬚⬚⬚⬚⬚

8. I minimize foods in my diet that contain large amounts of refined flour (Bleached white flour, typical store bread, cakes, etc.)

1 2 3 4 5
ANSWER = ⬚⬚⬚⬚⬚

9. I minimize my intake of fats and oils including margarine and animal fats.

1 2 3 4 5
ANSWER = ⬚⬚⬚⬚⬚

10. I avoid adding sugar to my food and I minimize my intake of presweetened foods such as sugar-coated cereals, syrups, chocolate milk, and most processed and fast foods.

1 2 3 4 5
ANSWER = ⬚⬚⬚⬚⬚

1 2 3 4 5
TOTAL = ⬚⬚⬚⬚⬚

Self Care

Check. 1 = almost always 2 = very frequently 3 = frequently
4 = occasionally   5 = almost never

1 2 3 4 5
ANSWER = ⬚⬚⬚⬚⬚

1. I maintain an up-to-date immunization record.

1 2 3 4 5
ANSWER = ⬚⬚⬚⬚⬚

2. I examine my breasts or testes on a monthly basis.

1 2 3 4 5
ANSWER = ⬚⬚⬚⬚⬚

3. I take action to minimize my exposure to tobacco smoke.

1 2 3 4 5
ANSWER = ⬚⬚⬚⬚⬚

4. When I'm experiencing illness or injury, I take necessary steps to correct the problem.

1 2 3 4 5
ANSWER = ⬚⬚⬚⬚⬚

5. I brush my teeth after eating.

1 2 3 4 5
ANSWER = ⬚⬚⬚⬚⬚

6. I floss my teeth after eating.

ANSWER = ☐☐☐☐☐ (1 2 3 4 5)

7. My resting pulse is 60 or less.

ANSWER = ☐☐☐☐☐ (1 2 3 4 5)

8. I get an adequate amount of sleep.

ANSWER = ☐☐☐☐☐ (1 2 3 4 5)

9. I keep my blood pressure in a range that minimizes my chances of disease. (e.g. stroke, heart attack and kidney disease)

ANSWER = ☐☐☐☐☐ (1 2 3 4 5)

10. I keep my cholesterol level, high density lipids and triglycerides in a range that minimizes my chances of disease.

ANSWER = ☐☐☐☐☐ (1 2 3 4 5)

TOTAL = ☐☐☐☐☐ (1 2 3 4 5)

Drugs and Driving

Questions 1 through 9.
Check. 1 = strongly agree 2 = agree 3 = neutral/not sure
4 = disagree 5 = strongly disagree

1. I do not operate vehicles under the influence of alcohol or other drugs.

ANSWER = ☐☐☐☐☐ (1 2 3 4 5)

2. I do not ride with vehicle operators who are under the influence of alcohol or other drugs.

ANSWER = ☐☐☐☐☐ (1 2 3 4 5)

3. I stay within the speed limit.

ANSWER = ☐☐☐☐☐ (1 2 3 4 5)

4. I maintain a safe driving distance between cars based on speed.

ANSWER = ☐☐☐☐☐ (1 2 3 4 5)

5. Vehicles which I drive are maintained to assure safety.

ANSWER = ☐☐☐☐☐ (1 2 3 4 5)

6. I avoid the use of tobacco.

ANSWER = [1 2 3 4 5]

7. I do not consume more than two alcoholic drinks per day.

ANSWER = [1 2 3 4 5]

8. I avoid using drugs obtained from unlicensed sources.

ANSWER = [1 2 3 4 5]

9. I consider alternatives to drugs.

ANSWER = [1 2 3 4 5]

10. I follow the instructions provided with any drug I take.
    1 = almost always   2 = very frequently   3 = frequently
    4 = occasionally   5 = almost never

ANSWER = [1 2 3 4 5]

TOTAL = [1 2 3 4 5]

Social

Check.   1 = strongly agree   2 = agree   3 = neutral/not sure
           4 = disagree   5 = strongly disagree

1. I take steps to conserve energy in my place of residence.

ANSWER = [1 2 3 4 5]

2. I contribute to the feeling of acceptance within my family.

ANSWER = [1 2 3 4 5]

3. When I see a safety hazard, I take action (warn others or correct
   the problem).

ANSWER = [1 2 3 4 5]

4. I avoid unnecessary radiation.

ANSWER = [1 2 3 4 5]

5. I contribute time and/or money to community projects.

ANSWER = [1 2 3 4 5]

6. I use my creativity in constructive ways.

ANSWER = [1 2 3 4 5]

7. My behavior reflects fairness and justice.

ANSWER = [1 2 3 4 5]

8. When possible, I choose an environment which is free of noise pollution.

ANSWER = [1 2 3 4 5]

9. When possible, I choose an environment which is free of air pollution.

ANSWER = [1 2 3 4 5]

10. I do my part to promote clean air.

ANSWER = [1 2 3 4 5]

TOTAL = [1 2 3 4 5]

Emotional Awareness

Questions 1 through 8.
Check. 1 = strongly agree 2 = agree 3 = neutral/not sure
         4 = disagree   5 = strongly disagree

1. I am comfortable in my relationships with others.

ANSWER = [1 2 3 4 5]

2. I feel positive about myself.

ANSWER = [1 2 3 4 5]

3. I feel there is an appropriate amount of excitement in my life.

ANSWER = [1 2 3 4 5]

4. My emotional life is stable.

ANSWER = [1 2 3 4 5]

5. When I make mistakes, I learn from them.

ANSWER = [1 2 3 4 5]

6. I feel enthusiastic about my life.

ANSWER = [1 2 3 4 5]

7. I find it easy to laugh.

ANSWER = ☐☐☐☐☐ (1 2 3 4 5)

8. I enjoy my life.

ANSWER = ☐☐☐☐☐ (1 2 3 4 5)

9. I have plenty of energy.
   1 = almost always 2 = very frequently 3 = frequently
   4 = occasionally   5 = almost never

ANSWER = ☐☐☐☐☐ (1 2 3 4 5)

10. My sleep is restful.
    1 = almost always 2 = very frequently 3 = frequently
    4 = occasionally   5 = almost never

ANSWER = ☐☐☐☐☐ (1 2 3 4 5)

TOTAL = ☐☐☐☐☐ (1 2 3 4 5)

Emotional Control

Questions 1 through 5.
Check. 1 = strongly agree 2 = agree 3 = neutral/not sure
        4 = disagree   5 = strongly disagree

1. I can express my feelings of anger.

ANSWER = ☐☐☐☐☐ (1 2 3 4 5)

2. I can say 'NO' without feeling guilty.

ANSWER = ☐☐☐☐☐ (1 2 3 4 5)

3. I make decisions with a minimum of stress and worry.

ANSWER = ☐☐☐☐☐ (1 2 3 4 5)

4. There is an appropriate amount of time urgency in my daily routine.

ANSWER = ☐☐☐☐☐ (1 2 3 4 5)

5. I include relaxation time as part of my daily routine.

ANSWER = ☐☐☐☐☐ (1 2 3 4 5)

Questions 6 through 10.
Check. 1 = almost always 2 = very frequently 3 = frequently
        4 = occasionally   5 = almost never

6. I am able to develop close, intimate relationships.

ANSWER = [1 2 3 4 5]

7. I set realistic objectives for myself.

ANSWER = [1 2 3 4 5]

8. I can relax my body and mind (without using drugs).

ANSWER = [1 2 3 4 5]

9. I accept responsibility for my actions.

ANSWER = [1 2 3 4 5]

10. I accept the responsibility for creating my own feelings.

ANSWER = [1 2 3 4 5]

TOTAL = [1 2 3 4 5]

Intellectual

Check. 1 = strongly agree 2 = agree 3 = neutral/not sure
         4 = disagree   5 = strongly disagree

1. I keep abreast of social and political issues.

ANSWER = [1 2 3 4 5]

2. I am interested in learning about scientific discoveries.

ANSWER = [1 2 3 4 5]

3. I make an effort to maintain and improve my verbal skills.

ANSWER = [1 2 3 4 5]

4. I make an effort to maintain and improve my writing skills.

ANSWER = [1 2 3 4 5]

5. I am satisfied with the entertainment choices I make.

ANSWER = [1 2 3 4 5]

6. I carefully select my movies and television choices.

ANSWER = [1 2 3 4 5]

7. I maintain a continuing education program relative to my career.

1 2 3 4 5
ANSWER = ☐☐☐☐☐

8. I am satisfied with the amount and variety I read.

1 2 3 4 5
ANSWER = ☐☐☐☐☐

9. It's easy for me to apply knowledge gained in one situation to a new situation.

1 2 3 4 5
ANSWER = ☐☐☐☐☐

10. I am interested in understanding the view of others.

1 2 3 4 5
ANSWER = ☐☐☐☐☐

1 2 3 4 5
TOTAL = ☐☐☐☐☐

Occupational

Check.   1 = strongly agree   2 = agree   3 = neutral/not sure
4 = disagree   5 = strongly disagree

1. I enjoy my work.

1 2 3 4 5
ANSWER = ☐☐☐☐☐

2. I take advantage of opportunities to learn new skills in my work.

1 2 3 4 5
ANSWER = ☐☐☐☐☐

3. My work is challenging.

1 2 3 4 5
ANSWER = ☐☐☐☐☐

4. I feel my job responsibilities are consistent with my values.

1 2 3 4 5
ANSWER = ☐☐☐☐☐

5. I look forward to doing my job.

1 2 3 4 5
ANSWER = ☐☐☐☐☐

6. I am satisfied with the balance between my work time and leisure time.

1 2 3 4 5
ANSWER = ☐☐☐☐☐

7. I am satisfied with my ability to plan my workload.

1 2 3 4 5
ANSWER = ☐☐☐☐☐

8. I receive adequate feedback to judge my work performance.

ANSWER =

1 2 3 4 5

9. To the extent that I can, I create an environment which minimizes my stress.

ANSWER =

1 2 3 4 5

10. To the extent that I can, I create an environment which minimizes the stress at my organizational level or other levels.

ANSWER =

1 2 3 4 5

TOTAL =

1 2 3 4 5

Spiritual

Check. 1 = strongly agree 2 = agree 3 = neutral/not sure

4 = disagree 5 = strongly disagree

1. I am satisfied with my spiritual life.

ANSWER =

1 2 3 4 5

2. Prayer, meditation, and/or quiet personal reflection is/are important part(s) of my life.

ANSWER =

1 2 3 4 5

3. My values guide my daily life.

ANSWER =

1 2 3 4 5

4. My spiritual growth is an important lifelong process.

ANSWER =

1 2 3 4 5

5. I am concerned about humanitarian issues.

ANSWER =

1 2 3 4 5

6. I participate in discussions about spiritual values.

ANSWER =

1 2 3 4 5

7. Contemplating my purpose in life is an important issue for me.

ANSWER =

1 2 3 4 5

8. I am satisfied with the degree to which my job is consistent with my values.

ANSWER =
1	2	3	4	5

9. I am satisfied with the degree to which my leisure time activities are consistent with my values.

ANSWER =
1	2	3	4	5

10. I am tolerant of the values and beliefs of others.

ANSWER =
1	2	3	4	5

TOTAL =
1	2	3	4	5

Self-Scoring System*

For each section count how many

1's ____ × 10 =
2's ____ × 8 =
3's ____ × 6 =
4's ____ × 4 =
5's ____ × 2 =

TOTAL _____

Your average of all sections is your composite score.

Sample Printout

Example:

SECTION	PERCENT OF POINTS
Physical Fitness	100
Physical—Nutritional	100
Physical—Self-Care	90
Drugs and Driving	94
Social—Environment	86
Emotional Awareness	44
Emotional Control	86
Intellectual	100
Occupational	100
Spiritual	100

*This questionnaire is also available on IBM Compatible Microcomputer Software.

*** COMPOSITE SCORE ***   90

*** What do these percents mean? ***

90–100%	EXCELLENT—Super Job!
80– 89%	GOOD—Better than most
70– 79%	AVERAGE—Mediocrity is ok, but?
60– 69%	FAIR—Reassess your present lifestyle
Less than 60%	POOR—Are you really trying?

APPENDIX C

Selected Colleges and Universities Offering Academic Wellness Programs

University of Georgia
Harry P. Duval, Ph.D.
Director
Fitness Center
Physical Education Building
University of Georgia
Athens, GA 30602

Georgia State University
Dr. G. Rankin Cooter, Director
Physical Fitness Center
Georgia State University
Altanta, GA 30303

Mankato State University
Joseph Hogan, Ph.D.
Mankato State University
Mankato, MN 56001

University of Nebraska-Lincoln
Leon H. Rottman, Ph.D.
120C Leverton Hall
University of Nebraska
Lincoln, NB 68583

Northeastern University
Marilyn A. Cairns, Ph.D.
Department of Physical Education
Northeastern University
360 Huntington Avenue
Boston, MA 02115

University of North Florida
Dr. Terry R. Tabor, Coordinator
Health Promotion Track
COEHS
University of North Florida
Jacksonville, FL 32216

Peabody College of Vanderbilt
    University
Sharon L. Shields, Ph.D.
Department of Physical Education
Box 330
Peabody College
Vanderbilt University
Nashville, TN 37203

Purdue University
Dr. Gerald C. Hyner
Department of PEHRS
106 Lambert
Purdue University
West Lafayette, IN 47907

Southeast Missouri State University
Joan McPherson, Ph.D.
Parker Hall
Southeast Missouri State University
Cape Girardeau, MO 63701

Springfield College
Dr. William J. Considine, Chair
Physical Education and Health/
   Fitness
Springfield College
Springfield, MA 01109

St. Cloud State University
John M. Kelly, DPE
Dept. of Health, Physical Education
   and Recreation
St. Cloud State University
St. Cloud, MN 56301

University of Wisconsin-Stevens
   Point
Alice Clawson, Ph.D.
Associate Dean and Head
School of Health, Physical Education,
   Recreation and Athletics
University of Wisconsin-Stevens
   Point
Stevens Point, WI 54481

Youngstown State University
Dr. Tony Whitney
Dept. of Health and Physical
   Education
Youngstown State University
410 Wick Avenue
Youngstown, OH 44555

APPENDIX D

Examples of University of Wisconsin-Stevens Point Wellness Programs by Wellness Dimension and Department

I. PHYSICAL DIMENSION

   A. Health Center
      1. SHAC programs
         a. Stress management
         b. Physical fitness
         c. Nutrition
         d. Contraception
         e. Blood pressure monitoring and control
         f. Dental wellness
      2. Sponsor regular functions
      3. LAQ
      4. Class on medical self-care

   B. Student Life Activities and Programs
      1. Diet education
      2. Nutrition alternatives in dining centers
      3. Outdoor recreation
      4. Fifteen (15) student organizations dealing with physical dimensions
      5. Intramural programs liaison
      6. Athletic programs liaison

   C. University Centers
      1. Recreation equipment rental
      2. Handicapped facilities
      3. Indoor recreation
      4. Advocate safety

      D. Counseling Center
1. Body tune-up group (weight loss)
2. Non-smoking group
3. Relaxation and biofeedback training

      E. Residence Life
1. Several wellness clubs and fitness programs
2. Weight lifting and exercise rooms including saunas
3. Advocate of intramurals
4. Advocate safety

      F. Business Operations
1. Environment and interior design
2. Advocate safety

      G. Special Activities
Dance Marathon, Don Ardell, George Sheehan

II. EMOTIONAL DIMENSION

      A. Counseling
1. Individual counseling
2. Relationship couples and premarriage consultation
3. Assertiveness, personal growth groups
4. Alcoholism group
5. Alcohol education thrust
6. Crisis intervention component
7. Employee assistance program
8. Psychological assessment & evaluation
9. Dial help
10. Individual presentations to public
11. Newspaper articles

      B. Health
1. One to one and referral
2. Videotape library
3. Presentations
4. Newspaper articles

      C. Residence Life
1. SDTI interpretation
2. LAQ interpretation
3. Hall and wing programs
4. Human development programs
5. Individual consultation
6. Some attempts at topical months or weeks
7. Hall council advising

      8. Human development programs
      9. Private environment
    10. Numerous opportunities for involvement and success

  D. Student Life Activities & Programs
      1. Volunteer service learning ·
      2. Leadership training
      3. Advising to student organization leadership

  E. University Centers
      1. Student manager program
      2. Private environments

III. OCCUPATIONAL—VOCATIONAL

  A. Counseling
      1. Career information resources
      2. Vocational assessment
      3. Individual counseling
      4. Resource person card file
      5. Career planning group
      6. Task force for decision making and vocation program thrust among various units
      7. FACTS involvement

  B. Residence Life
      1. Several career rooms
      2. Hall council and other government and program leadership
      3. Resident assistant program
      4. Career and vocational individual consultation
      5. Student labor training

  C. Student Life Activities & Programs
      1. Volunteer service learning
      2. Twenty (20) student organizations that are career oriented
      3. Leadership skills workshops
      4. Student staff

  D. University Centers
      1. Student managers
      2. Food service managers and student labor
      3. Individual consultation
      4. Maintain placement possibilities
      5. Recently begun maintaining transcript of experiences
      6. Arts and crafts center
      7. Student staff in all center areas

IV. SPIRITUAL DIMENSION

    A. Counseling
       1. Value clarification experiences
       2. Individual consultation

    B. Residence Life
       1. Student workshops
       2. Human development programs
       3. RA training
       4. Coordination with campus ministries
       5. Discipline
       6. Contracts for change

    C. Student Life Activities & Programs
       1. Fifteen (15) student organizations dealing with spiritual values or religious beliefs
       2. Volunteer/service-learning experiences
       3. Schmeeckle reserve liaison with students

    D. General—Videotapes (Bascaglia, Kern, Sheehan)

    E. Student Conduct

V. SOCIAL

    A. Health
       1. SHAC sponsored gym all-nights; folk and square dancing, roller skating
       2. Support of Environmental Health & Safety Committee

    B. Counseling
       1. Marriage and family counseling
       2. Sexuality groups
       3. All group counseling sessions

    C. Student Life Activities & Programs
       1. Schmeeckle reserve liaison with students
       2. Student government association liaison
       3. Coordination and officer training of 130 student organizations
       4. Dining room environment
       5. 12–15 student "social" groups
       6. Activities and programs coordination of the different communities

D. Halls
   1. Emphasis on community
   2. Hall government
   3. Social activities
   4. Interior design thrust
   5. Custodial and maintenance programs
   6. Human development programs
   7. International program

E. Student Conduct

VI. INTELLECTUAL DIMENSION

A. Counseling
   1. Reading and study skills
   2. Testing (intelligence, aptitude, achievement)
   3. Academic advising
   4. Occasional course development

B. Health
   1. Teaching
   2. Course development
   3. Information dispersal (pamphlets) etc.
   4. Medical self-care

C. Residence Life
   1. Staff training
   2. Reading and study skills consultation
   3. Human development program
   4. International programs
   5. Staff training workshops
   6. Student growth workshops

D. University Center
   1. Materials centers
   2. Tutorial advocacy
   3. University store
   4. Arts & crafts center

E. Student Life Activities & Programs
   1. Coordinate with arts & lectures
   2. Teaching of skills & workshops
   3. Mini courses through UAE
   4. Ten student organizations dedicated to creative/
      intellectual pursuits

APPENDIX E

ORGANIZATIONAL HEALTH PROMOTION RESOURCE GUIDE

Adamson, G. J. Health promotion and wellness: A marketing strategy. *Group Practice Journal*, May/June 1981, 17–22.

AFB Action. Association for Fitness in Business, Stamford, Connecticut (monthly).

Allen, Robert F., and Kraft, Charlotte. *The Organizational Unconscious.* Englewood Cliffs, New Jersey: Prentice-Hall, Inc., 1982.

Ardell, Donald B., and Tager, Mark J. *Planning for Wellness.* Dubuque, IA: Kendall-Hunt Publishing Company, 1982.

Bader, Garry S., Jones, Lynn Dickey, and Yenny, Sharon. *Planning Hospital Health Promotion Services for Business and Industry.* Chicago, IL: American Hospital Association, 1982.

Beehr, T. A. Work-role stress and attitudes toward co-workers. *Group and Organization Studies*, June 1981, 6(2), 201–209.

Beehr, T. A., and Newman, J. E. Job stress, employee health, and organizational effectiveness: A facet analysis, model, and literature review. *Personnel Psychology*, Winter 1978, 31(4), 655–699.

Berry, Charles A. *Good Health for Employees and Reduced Health Care Costs for Industry.* Washington, D.C.: Health Insurance Association of America, 1981.

Breslow, L. A positive strategy for the nation's health. *Journal of the American Medical Association*, November 9, 1979, 242(19), 2093–2095.

Business Insurance. Chicago, Illinois (weekly).

Butler, Sandra D. *Resource Guide for Health and Fitness Program Development.* Minnesota Coalition on Health Care Costs, 1982.

Center. National Center for Health Education, New York, NY (5 times annually).

Corporate Commentary—Worksite Health Evaluation Report. Washington Business Group on Health, Washington, D.C. (Quarterly).

Corporate Fitness and Recreation. The journal of employee health and service programs. Brentwood Publishing Corporation, Los Angeles, California (monthly).

Danaher, B. S. Smoking cessation in occupational settings: State of the art report. *National Conference on Health Programs in Occupational Settings*. Washington, D.C.: Office of Health Information and Health Promotion, Department of Health, Education, and Welfare, January 17–19, 1979.

Daniels, C. E. *Correlates of Type A Coronary Prone Behavior in a Middle/Upper Management Population*. Third Annual Meeting, Society of Behavioral Medicine, March 3–5, 1982.

Debats, K. E. Industrial recreation programs: A new look at an old benefit. *Personnel Journal*, August 1981, 60(8), 620–627.

Employers' Health Costs Savings Letter. Health Resources Publishing, Wall Township, New Jersey (monthly).

Epstein, Arnold M., Begg, Colin B., and McNeil, Barbara J. The effects of group size on test ordering for hypertensive patients. *The New England Journal of Medicine*. 309:464–468, August 25, 1983.

Ferguson, Marilyn. *The Aquarian Conspiracy*. Los Angeles, CA: Houghton Mifflin Company, 1980.

Foreyt, J. P., Scott, L. W., and Gotto, A. M. Weight control and nutrition education programs in occupational settings. *National Conference on Health Promotion Programs in Occupational Settings*. Washington, D.C.: Office of Health Information and Health Promotion, Department of Health, Education, and Welfare, January 13–19, 1979.

Foreyt, J. P., Scott, L. W., and Gotto, A. M. Weight control and nutrition education programs in occupational settings. *Public Health Reports* 95:127–136 (1980).

Harvard Medical School Health Letter. Periodic health exams in perspective, July 1980, 1–4.

Health Care Cost Containment—1983. International Foundation of Employee Benefits, Brookfield, Wisconsin.

Healthline. The Robert A. McNeil Foundation for Health Education. San Mateo California (monthly).

Health Values: Achieving High Level Wellness. Charles B. Slack, Inc., Thorofare, New Jersey (bi-monthly).

Kotz, H. J., and Fielding, J. E., eds. *Health, Education and Promotion: Agenda for the Eighties*. Summary report of an insurance industry conference on health education and promotion, Atlanta, Georgia, March 16–18, 1980 (sponsored by the Health Insurance Association of America).

Levin, P. J., and Wolfson, J. Health care and American business. *New England Journal of Medicine*, July 24, 1982, 320.

Medical Benefits—The Medical and Economic Digest. Kelly Communications, Charlottesville, Virginia (bi-weekly).

MRFIT Research Group. *The Multiple Risk Factor Intervention Trial (MRFIT): Results after Four Years of Intervention*. Paper presented at the Conference on Epidemiology, Washington, D.C., March 27–29, 1981 (sponsored by the Council on Epidemiology of the American Heart Association).

Naisbitt, John. *Megatrends*. New York, NY: Warner Books Inc., 1982.

National Center for Health Statistics. Prevention profile by Golden, P. M., Wilson, R. W., and Kavet, J. *Health, United States, 1983*. DHHS (PHS), Pub. #84-1232. Washington, D.C.: U.S. Government Printing Office, December 1983.

National Center for Health Statistics. *Health, United States, 1983*. DHHS (PHS), Pub. #84-1232. Washington, D.C.: U.S. Government Printing Office, December 1983.

O'Donnell, Michael P., and Ainsworth, Thomas. *Health Promotion in the Workplace*. New York, NY: John Wiley and Sons, 1984.

Opatz, Joseph P., ed. *Wellness Promotion Stategies: Selected Proceedings of the Eighth Annual National Wellness Conference*. Stevens Point, WI: Institute for Lifestyle Improvement, 1984.

Parkinson, R. S., and Associates (eds.). *Managing Health Promotion in the Workplace: Guidelines for Implementation and Evaluation*. Palo Alto, CA: Mayfield Publishing Company, 1982.

Pelletier, Kenneth R. *Mind as Healer, Mind as Slayer: A Holistic Approach to Preventing Stress Disorders*. New York: Delacorte and Delta, 1977.

Pelletier, Kenneth R. *Corporate Health Promotion Programs*. Ongoing study of the California Nexus Foundation, San Francisco, 1983.

Pelletier, Kenneth R. *Healthy People in Unhealthy Places: Stress and Fitness at Work*. New York, NY: Delacorte, Delta, and Doubleday, 1984.

Pelletier, Kenneth R. *A PARCOURSE for Health Promotion in the Workplace: A Guide for Implementing Health Promotion Programs*. San Francisco, CA: The California Nexus Foundation, 1983.

President's Council on Physical Fitness and Sports. *Fitness in the Workplace*. Washington, D.C. 20201: 1982.

Toffler, Alvin. *The Third Wave*. New York, NY: Bantam Books, 1980.

U.S. Department of Health, Education and Welfare. *Healthy People: The Surgeon General's report on health promotion and disease prevention*. Department of Health, Education, and Welfare (PHS), Pub. #79-55071. Washington, D.C.: U.S. Government Printing Office, 1979.

U.S. Department of Health and Human Services. *Proceedings of the National Conference on Health Promotion Programs in Occupational Settings*. Washington, D.C.: U.S. Government Printing Office, 1979.

Wellness Perspectives. Organization of Wellness Networks—The Institute for Lifestyle Improvement, Stevens Point, Wisconsin (Quarterly).

Zuti, William B. *Fitness the Y's Way*. Rosemont, IL: YMCA of the USA, 1983.

REFERENCES

Ardell, Donald. The history and future of the wellness movement. *In* J. P. Opatz (ed.) *Wellness Promotion Strategies.* Dubuque, IA: Kendall/Hunt, 1984, p. 24.

Bader, Barry S. *Planning Health Promotion Services for Business and Industry.* Chicago, IL: American Hospital Association, 1982, p. 17.

Berry, Charles A. *Good Health for Employees and Reduced Costs for Industry.* Washington, D.C.: Health Insurance Corporation of America, 1981, pp. 16–21.

Bouchard, T. Field research methods: Interviewing, questionnaires, participant observation, systematic observation, unobtrusive measures. *In* M. D. Dunnette (ed.) *Handbook of Industrial and Organizational Psychology.* Chicago: Rand McNally, 1976.

Chadwick, Joseph H. Health behavior change at the worksite: A problem oriented analysis. *In* Parkinson *et al. Managing Health Promotion at the Worksite.* Palo Alto, CA: Mayfield, 1982, p. 149.

Coon, Thomas. *The Structure of Scientific Revolutions* (2nd edition). Chicago, IL: University of Chicago Press, 1970.

Duff, Jean F. and Fritts, Patricia J. Stress Management for the 80's. *Business and Health.* May 1984, p. 9.

Dunn Halpert L. *High Level Wellness.* Arlington, VA: Beatty, 1961.

French, Wendell L. *The Personnel Management Process.* Boston, MA: Houghton Mifflin, 1978, 3, pp. 16–17.

Goetz, Axel and Bernstein, James. Computer developments in health risk management. *Corporate Commentary.* June 1984, p. 26.

Goldberg, Rob. Working out at work. *Savvy.* December 1983, pp. 55–56.

Grove, Andrew S. *High Output Management.* Random House, NY: 1984.

Hackman, Richard J. Group influences on individuals. *In* Dunnette, M. D. (ed.) *Handbook of Industrial and Organizational Psychology.* Chicago, IL: Rand McNally, 1976, pp. 1455–1527.

Harvard Medical School Health Letter. Harvard Medical School. July 1980.

Huset, Richard. Cost containment strategies. Presentation at the *Health Promotion in the Organizational Setting Conference.* Minneapolis, MN: December 1983.

Johnson and Johnson. *Live for Life Program Technical Overview.* January 1983.

Kaplan, Robert M. The connection between clinical health promotion and health status. *American Psychologist.* July 1984, pp. 755–765.

Laser, William. *Marketing Management: A System Perspective.* New York, NY: John Wiley, 1971.

McClure, Walter. *Business and Health.* November 1983.

Miller, Theodore K. and Prince, Judith S. *The Future of Student Affairs.* San Francisco, CA: Jossey-Bass Inc., 1976, pp. 20–21.

Murphy, Colt L. Live for life: An epidemiological evaluation of a comprehensive health promotion program. Unpublished preliminary report on Johnson and Johnson *Live for Life* program. Fall 1983.

Murphy, Robert. Cost effectiveness of health promotion. Presentation at the National Wellness Conference. Stevens Point, WI: July 1984.

Peter, Thomas J. and Waterman, Robert H. Jr. *In search of excellence.* New York, NY: Harper and Row Inc., 1983, pp. 29–54.

Reiff, Theodore. An overview of human aging. *In* J. P. Opatz (ed.) *Wellness Promotion Strategies.* Dubuque, IA: Kendall/Hunt, 1984, pp. 73–93.

Scriven, Michael. The methodology of evaluation. *In* Worthen, B. R. and Sanders, J. R. (eds.) *Educational Evaluation: Theory and Practice.* Belmont, CA: Wadsworth Publishing Co., 1972, pp. 62–63.

Skinner, B. F. *Science and Human Behavior.* New York, NY: Macmillan Company, 1954.

Smith, H. W. *Strategies of Social Research.* Englewood Cliffs, NJ: Prentice Hall, 1975.

Tvedten, Jennifer. Final report of the Hennepin county breast self-examination program. *Hennepin County WellWay Program.* Unpublished report. 1983.

University of Wisconsin-Stevens Point. *Human Development Program: A Report to the University Planning Committee.* Unpublished report. Stevens Point, WI: November 1981.